ULTIMATE
BACKYARD

ULTIMATE
BACKYARD

INSPIRED IDEAS
FOR OUTDOOR LIVING

M I C H E L L E   K O D I S

Gibbs Smith, Publisher
Salt Lake City

For Rich

First Edition
10 09 08 07 06   5 4 3 2 1

Published by
Gibbs Smith, Publisher
P.O. Box 667
Layton, Utah 84041

Orders: 1.800.748.5439
www.gibbs-smith.com

Designed by Deibra McQuiston
Printed and bound in Hong Kong

Library of Congress Cataloging-in-Publication Data

Kodis, Michelle.
  Ultimate backyard : inspired ideas for outdoor living / Michelle Kodis.—
1st ed.
     p. cm.
  ISBN 1-58685-793-2
  1. Outdoor living spaces—Decoration—United States. 2. Landscape architecture. I. Title.

NK2117.O87K63 2006
712'.6—dc22

2005027275

Beautiful, soul-soothing outdoor spaces are for everyone.

CONTENTS

If you want to raise the value of your home, start thinking about its outdoor living spaces.

ACKNOWLEDGMENTS

Although writers spend a lot of time with just their thoughts for company, books are never written in isolation. I'd like to thank the following individuals for their contributions to this book.

The people at Gibbs Smith, Publisher, are an extraordinary crew. My deepest gratitude to Gibbs Smith, Suzanne Taylor, Christopher Robbins, Kurt Wahlner, Alison Einerson, Laura Ayrey, Hollie Keith, Carrie Westover, Anita Wood and Deibra McQuiston.

The photographers whose images grace these pages are enormously talented and generous with their time. I am very grateful to all of them but must give special mention to Claudio Santini. This is the fourth book of mine that features his photos, and I'm keeping my fingers crossed that we can work together again.

The architects and designers whose work makes this book what it is represent some of the most creative minds in the business. A number of them provided projects for my other books as well, and I appreciate their ongoing helpfulness and enthusiasm: John Sofio, Sintesi Design, Mark English, Scott Lindenau, KAA Design Group, Charles Bernstein, Ross Chapin and CCY Architects.

Then there are the friends and family members who offer support, advice, humor, lunch and mind-clearing walks in the mountains. Much love to Robert, Joan and Steven Kodis, the Cieciuch family, stepsons Andrew and Brett, and Stephen Cieciuch for taking my author photo. Rosemerry, beloved friend, you have stood by me in more ways than I can count. Finn Thilo, I love watching you grow. Kendall, Marcia, Donna, Susan S., Ramona, Anne, Susan V., Kierstin, Pam and Maureen—thank you for your friendship. And of course pats on the head to Violet and Roscoe.

My husband, Rich Cieciuch, gracefully accepts the challenges of being married to a writer and really is my biggest fan. He also offers commentary on content, suggestions for projects to include and technical clarification when I need it. Add to that a beautiful office in which to work, a beautiful house in which to live and as much freedom as I need. It's the stuff of dreams.

Backyards can reveal a sensitive response to a site
and showcase ways to enhance the sensory aspects
of the outdoor experience.

INTRODUCTION

What is more fundamental to the human spirit than the need to connect to nature? As we become an increasingly harried and technologically driven society, many of us develop an even greater longing for the solace of a forest, the sound of a waterfall, the tapestry of a sunset. If you, too, feel this desire beginning to well up, it doesn't mean you have to move to the country or seclude yourself on the top of a mountain. As you will see in this book, there are many wonderful ways to strengthen your relationship to the outdoors, and it doesn't matter where you live or how much money you have. Beautiful, soul-soothing outdoor spaces are for everyone, and this book was written with that thought firmly in mind.

My goal when researching and writing this book was to present dwellings that connect to their sites primarily through their architecture. There is a common thread here, and it's pretty straightforward: great contemporary design. The backyards and outdoor spaces featured in these pages all reveal a sensitive response to the site and showcase ways to enhance the sensory aspects of the outdoor experience.

The other benefit, perhaps not as romantic but equally legitimate, is financial. As more and more people seek to improve their outdoor spaces, whether a small patio or the side of a mountain, they know that doing so would be a wise investment in their overall property. If you want to raise the value of your home, start thinking

about ways to add structural interest and comfort to your backyard, patio, deck, side yard—you name it. You'll find plenty of ideas for doing so in this book's thirty-seven chapters, which together offer a spectrum of examples of outdoor spaces designed for all kinds of budgets and in a variety of locales, all with an emphasis on contemporary design and materiality.

The chapters are divided into four sections: *Outdoor Rooms, Indoor/Outdoor Connections, Water,* and *Creative Landscapes.* In *Outdoor Rooms,* you will read about outdoor spaces that have been transformed into stylish, inviting rooms. In *Indoor/Outdoor Connections,* the focus shifts to outdoor spaces that are extensions of the interiors and which reflect the architecture and materiality of the house. In *Water,* you will find outdoor spaces that incorpo-

rate water features or use water as the focal point of the design. And, in *Creative Landscapes,* you will discover outdoor spaces that go far beyond the ordinary to connect a home and its people to the setting, whether urban, suburban or rural.

This book was a joy to research and write. As I delved into the chapters, I began to feel an unexpected sense of intimacy with the homes I was writing about. It struck me one day that I was reacting to this common longing for a bit of green in our lives, tranquility after a busy day, the scent of flowers, peacefulness in difficult times, a place for play. As I took in the mountain views framed by my office windows, I smiled often, glad to share in this united passion for the power and grace of the natural world, and for thoughtful architecture that facilitates this all-important connection.

Humans share a passion for the power and grace of the natural world, and for thoughtful architecture and design that facilitate a connection to nature.

Outdoor Rooms

OREGON COAST COTTAGE
Design: Tim Gordon, Boora Architects
Photographs: Sally Schoolmaster

Challenge: Comfortable outdoor spaces in a climate characterized by power-ful coastal winds and rain, and a way to make a small house feel bigger.

Result: A house that embraces the ocean views and incorporates protected outdoor rooms into its design.

This charming Oregon Coast house is just 1,500 square feet in size, but its generously appointed outdoor rooms nearly double the living space.

Designed by architect Tim Gordon for his mother, Leslie, the house has a duality that responds to the site and takes into account local weather patterns. On the east-side entry, the house turns in on itself, shielding a lovingly tended garden from the coastal winds; on the west side, which overlooks the ocean, large windows and sliding glass doors connect the living room to a 1,000-square-foot covered deck. Windows at the front entry lead the eye through the house, toward the deck and to the ocean view beyond.

One of Gordon's biggest challenges was creating comfortable outdoor rooms in what can be an unruly climate. His strategy involved building layers of protection from the elements right into the house and surrounding property. For example, the roof is equipped with three-foot overhangs on all sides, and the sweeping deck overhang accommodates gatherings even when it's raining. Heeding his mother's requests for a garden that she could enjoy year-round and a sitting area away from the deck, Gordon created a series of little outdoor rooms on

FACING ABOVE: The front of the house wraps around a private garden and sitting area, while the back opens to ocean views. The main exterior materials are white cedar shingles, red cedar siding and asphalt roofing, all good choices for a coastal climate.

The architect chose six shades of asphalt to create a roof-shingle pattern that is more visually interesting than a solid color.

FACING BELOW: The back of the house opens to a large deck that functions as an outdoor room. The deck railing, made from tube steel set into a cedar frame, gently encloses the space without blocking views. The deck can be closed off by gates that match the railing, forming a safe place for kids and pets.

ABOVE: The dining section of the deck is protected by a substantial overhang that extends from the house at an angle that shields the table from rain. The architect chose weather-resistant cedar for the deck floor. The owner's dog, Mali, can stay outside unaccompanied when the deck gates are closed.

the more sheltered sides of the house. The windows on the east façade frame views of the garden's terrace, rock walls, flower beds, tiny patch of lawn and small pond.

The architect also considered the weather when selecting exterior materials, opting for durable cedar siding and decking and long-lasting asphalt roof shingles arranged in a mosaic of soft greys.

Gordon's meticulous arrangement of indoor and outdoor rooms has connected the house to its landscape in a manner that offers the best of both worlds: a spacious deck for entertaining and a secluded garden for quieter, more introspective moments. "This blending of the interiors and exteriors is what makes the outdoor rooms successful," he says. "Every room in the house relates in some way to the environment around it."

ABOVE: A smaller outdoor room on the more sheltered garden side of the house includes a concrete block built-in bench that forms a nook for a table.

FACING ABOVE LEFT: The built-in bench is inset with a cedar seating platform covered with cushions made by the owner.

FACING ABOVE RIGHT: A cedar-enclosed outdoor shower is easily accessed from the back deck and is perfect for rinsing off after a day at the beach. The shower is partially covered by one of the three-foot overhangs present on all sides of the house.

FACING BELOW: The deck side of the house features a wall of windows designed to frame the ocean views. Sliding glass doors allow the living room to flow straight out onto the deck.

URBAN OASIS

Design: Rick Harlan Schneider, Inscape Studio
Photographs: Dan Redmond, Stephanie Gross and Inscape Studio

Challenge: A tiny urban backyard with limited opportunities for gardening or entertaining, and an awkward connection to the house.

Result: An outdoor room with walls that accommodate a vertical garden, and a new configuration between the indoors and outdoors.

Many city dwellers face this very challenge: What to do with a diminutive outdoor space in an urban setting? Architect Rick Harlan Schneider's solution for a client who enjoys gardening was to introduce vertical possibilities that free up the ground for other uses.

As he embarked on a remodel of his 1,200-square-foot circa-1900 townhome in downtown Washington, D.C., the owner listed his desires for his new yard: a three-season outdoor room suited to informal gatherings, and—a top priority—a place to garden.

After analyzing the house and noting its clumsy, seven-step-down connection to the backyard via an old metal stair, Schneider proposed a cost-effective and sustainable solution that would meet his client's needs without requiring a major structural overhaul. He replaced the original single door with wide glass doors that, when open, obscure the boundary between inside and out, a visual effect further enhanced with a transom and side windows. He removed the metal stair, raised the yard

floor, and formed a private outdoor room enclosed with sustainably harvested cedar fences that double as "green" walls with trellises, hanging flower boxes and a row of planters on top of the fence. "Why a vertical garden? If you don't have the room on the ground, go up," the architect points out. Candles in perforated metal holders attached to the walls can be lit at night, and when the evenings turn cool, a fireplace warms the space. A dining table and cushioned bench provide a comfortable place to gather.

"The small size of this urban backyard was not necessarily detrimental," Schneider concludes. "It allowed for a very creative approach and solution, and that is what is fun about situations like this: you can look at things not as limitations but as opportunities. In this case, the owner gets to live in the city and also exercise his green thumb."

FACING ABOVE LEFT: Before the remodel, the circa-1900 townhouse, located in a historic Washington, D.C., neighborhood, presented limited opportunities for outdoor living. Photo by Inscape Studio.

FACING ABOVE RIGHT: An operable side window in the kitchen encourages natural ventilation and enhances the connection between the interior and exterior. Turning the walls into vertical "gardens" freed up the ground for other uses. Photo by Dan Redmond.

FACING BELOW: The outdoor room is hidden behind sustainably harvested cedar walls that support planters, which ring the yard in greenery. Photo by Inscape Studio.

ABOVE: French doors in the reconfigured kitchen open directly to the yard, which prior to the remodel sat at the bottom of a rickety stair. The architect raised the yard floor for direct indoor/outdoor access. Photo by Dan Redmond.

RIGHT: The room glows at night, thanks to candles held in perforated metal holders fastened to the walls. Photo by Stephanie Gross.

BELOW LEFT: For owner Scott Sanders, pictured here, the outdoor room is a quiet place to read and enjoy the outdoors—even in this energetic urban neighborhood. The glass doors are argon-filled double-insulated low-E panes. Photo by Stephanie Gross.

BELOW RIGHT: A custom fireplace/barbecue, dining table and cushioned bench make the space a true outdoor room. The patio is clad in stone from a local quarry. Photo by Inscape Studio.

FACING: The fireplace can be used to warm the room during cool weather. Photo by Dan Redmond.

A Sense of Discovery

Design: Bill Nicholas, Nicholas Budd Dutton Architects

Photographs: Claudio Santini

Challenge: Organize a large yard into outdoor rooms with defined functions and architectural ties to the house.

Result: A series of thematically linked spaces that together form a unified outdoor room that feels like an extension of the house.

The architect of this Los Angeles home took advantage of the mild year-round climate and a spacious site to create outdoor rooms with defined functions joined by complementary forms and materials.

With three large terraces, two covered porches, a pool surrounded by a lawn, a fireplace, a barbecue and three fountains, the home, designed by architect Bill Nicholas, gives the owners an array of outdoor living possibilities. For Nicholas, consistency between the indoors and outdoors was key. "It was important to make a physical connection between the interior and outdoor rooms, so that the spaces as a whole would be continuous," he points out. "The interiors of this house seem to extend out into the yard, and that was accomplished with adjacent outdoor areas that have a corollary to the interiors."

The outdoor spaces do appear as extensions of the house, both in their design and elegant materiality. The yard is divided by structural elements that relate to the building, and organized into zones for privacy or social gatherings. "The overall effect is one of discovery as you move through the yard," Nicholas points out. "From inside, you have either carefully framed views of the outdoor spaces or direct access to them."

The owners didn't want a fussy, high-maintenance yard but did desire a landscape full of texture and color. In one section of the garden, for example, a low-maintenance lavender grove brings a broad sweep of color to the setting and contrasts well with the more formal lines of the masonry wood-burning fireplace.

The home's main exterior materials—smooth trowel finish stucco and redwood siding—are subdued, a design strategy that places the emphasis on the architecture itself.

TOP: The house features smooth trowel finish stucco, redwood siding and a metal roof.

ABOVE: The house engages with the courtyard patio, thanks to doors and windows that visually and physically connect the indoor and outdoor spaces. The patio is Utah sandstone.

FACING: The outdoor rooms extend from the house in an organized, almost formal manner, with an emphasis on complementary materials and straightforward indoor/outdoor access.

ABOVE: The wood-burning masonry fireplace is anchored by a matching garden wall, and an adjacent barbecue makes outdoor cooking enjoyable and easy.

RIGHT: A covered porch doubles as an outdoor reading room. The opening in the wall connects the room to the garden without compromising the private qualities of the space.

LEFT: A low-maintenance lavender garden brings color and texture to the yard and helps balance the masonry wall and fireplace.

ABOVE: Fixed mahogany louvers shade the interiors without blocking views to the garden.

BELOW LEFT: There are three fountains on the property, including this custom design that recirculates water through a piece of copper pipe embedded in the wall.

THINKING OUT OF THE BOX

Design: José Fontiveros and Mariana Boctor, Sintesi Design
Photographs: Claudio Santini

Challenge: A small backyard with limited opportunities for an outdoor living space, and the desire for a modern update to a 1950s house.

Result: A self-contained and integrated canopy structure that appears to emerge directly from the house to form a covered deck with a built-in couch.

A request for a remodel with a modern sensibility and a revamping of the small backyard of this southern California house prompted architects José Fontiveros and Mariana Boctor to literally think out of the box.

The project occurred in two phases that now speak the same architectural language. The first was a remodel of the yard-side master bedroom and bathroom. To forge a visual and physical connection to the yard, the architects placed a new ground-level soaking tub into a glass box enclosure, then covered the box with thin teak louvers for privacy and sun protection. The box, supported by a steel frame, pops out of the bathroom wall and one of its panels pivots open, making it possible, if desired, to step out of the tub and straight into the yard.

The first phase completed, the architects moved on to the task of creating an outdoor living area that would have minimal impact on the house and not overwhelm the compact yard. Taking their cues from the tub enclosure, the architects designed a U-shaped redwood canopy that cantilevers out over the yard at the living

LEFT: Thin teak louvers attached to the steel frame of the floor-to-ceiling tub enclosure prevent it from overheating in the sun. A full-height pivot window provides unimpeded views and access to the yard.

ABOVE: Opening the panel makes the bathtub enclosure feel like an outdoor room. The tub is clad in bluestone slate.

FACING: The U-shaped canopy forms a trellis and built-in couch and then wraps around to complete the deck. Made from redwood, the one-piece structure is held in place with two sturdy overhead beams, and a glass panel suspended beneath the trellis helps shield the doors from rain. A reflecting pond beneath the couch balances the strong lines of the deck.

room wall, forming a trellis overhead, a built-in couch on one
side, and wrapping around to
create a deck—all accomplished
with one connected piece. The
existing French doors were
replaced with two large Douglas
fir pivot doors which, when
open, turn the living room and
deck into an uninterrupted space.
"The idea was that the entire
structure, including the bathroom addition, have a lightness
and transparency that in turn
gives the house and yard simple
but clear transitions and connections," Fontiveros explains.

The architects also installed a
reflecting pool beneath the
built-in couch, which appears to
hover over the water. A glass
panel suspended beneath the
trellis with stainless steel hard-
ware protects the doors from
rain without visually intruding
into the structure. And, for additional color and texture and a
low-maintenance alternative to
turf, the architects installed
square concrete pavers and
divided them with dark pebbles.

FACING: When open, the wide Douglas fir pivot doors make the living room and deck seem like a contiguous space.

ABOVE: Owner Aura Kuperberg, pictured here, uses the outdoor room year-round. Two large pivot doors open the living room to the deck and newly configured outdoor space. The architects wanted the couch to appear to hover above the reflecting pond.

SANCTUARY ON A BUSY STREET

Design: Matt Charlot

Photographs: Matt Charlot and Marcus Hanschen

Challenge: A request for a budget-conscious outdoor room addition to a house located on a busy four-lane street and bordered on two sides by neighbors.

Result: An outdoor room enclosed by tall walls made from salvaged redwood and constructed using an affordable sound-proofing technique that effectively blocks noise.

This outdoor room reveals what can be accomplished in a particularly challenging environment. Here we see that a peaceful exterior living area is possible even when an urban street is just steps away.

The house is across from a former trolley line in Oakland, California. The trolley is gone, having been replaced with a clamorous four-lane thoroughfare. Wanting to be able to relax outside without being engulfed by the drone of passing motor traffic, the owner hired landscape designer Matt Charlot to create a haven amid the commotion.

As if the street weren't problem enough, the house also has neighbors on two sides. Charlot realized from the get-go that sound-proofing had to be the priority. To accomplish this—and on a budget—he enclosed the space with an eight-foot-high redwood-paneled fence that has two sheets of marine-grade plywood sandwiched into its framing, an affordable sound-deadening technique that in this case brought an added benefit: an even greater solidity to the structure. Says Charlot, "You feel safe and protected in the room because there's a real density to the walls."

RIGHT: Redwood, which resists rot and termites, was in this case very affordable because the designer used salvaged wood throughout the structure. He even turned the wood from an existing fence removed during construction into custom planters. Photo by Marcus Hanschen.

FACING: Alcoves built into the fence walls are a space-conscious way to display art. The ambience of the outdoor room is enhanced with low-voltage lighting in the alcoves and a chandelier over the table. Photo by Matt Charlot.

There are no gaps anywhere, so the area is completely enclosed and separate from the setting beyond it."

Hidden from the street and the neighbors, the space has the appeal of an outdoor living room. Alcoves back up against the plywood, forming niches for displaying pieces of the owner's art collection. The alcoves are wired with low-voltage directional spotlights and a functional chandelier hangs over a small table. A redwood trellis overhead helps to further contain and define the room and will eventually support a vine. The owner had requested a hot tub but there wasn't enough room for it. In its place, Charlot installed an outdoor shower. The owner uses the shower frequently, thrilled that his urban outdoor room allows him to do so in complete privacy.

FACING: Flagstone patio pavers complement the rusticity of the redwood used for the room. The outdoor shower is tucked into a corner of the space and protected by an overhead trellis, which will eventually support a vine. Photo by Marcus Hanschen.

ABOVE: Enclosed in a stall made from salvaged redwood, the outdoor shower is used frequently by the owner, who doesn't have to worry about privacy thanks to the height of the enclosure walls. Photo by Marcus Hanschen.

RIGHT: The home's urban setting made noise reduction and privacy imperative. Both goals were achieved with tall redwood-paneled walls inset with double sheets of sound-deadening marine-grade plywood. Photo by Marcus Hanschen.

OUTDOOR ROOM FOR A FAMILY

Design: Michelle Van de Voorde, Elemental Design
Photographs: Gregory Case

Challenge: A low-maintenance, multifunctional outdoor room that can comfortably accommodate gatherings of adults and kids.

Result: A year-round space with separate zones for play, relaxation, outdoor cooking and dining, and a selection of materials and plants that require minimal upkeep.

The owners of this outdoor room in San Mateo, California, had specific goals in mind when they hired landscape architect Michelle Van de Voorde to redesign their backyard.

"They have teenage sons on the football team, and a young child," Van de Voorde explains. "Important to them was a play space that wouldn't turn into a muddy mess every time the kids staged a football game. And, they have an extended family that they invite over often for gatherings, so their outdoor space needed to work on a variety of levels, whether the focus was on cooking, entertaining, relaxing or playing—or everything together."

Working with limited square footage, potentially problematic drainage issues and the request that the yard be as low-maintenance as possible, Van de Voorde drew a site plan that organizes the yard into three distinct zones on two terraced levels divided by a concrete retaining wall. The lower terrace houses an outdoor kitchen, placed beneath an overhang for protection and conveniently accessed from the interior kitchen through a sliding window; a dining patio; a canopy-covered seating area; and a fountain. The upper terrace, designed for the kids, has a playhouse equipped with a climbing wall and sports court. Rather than a traditional lawn, Van de Voorde opted for synthetic turf, which solved the mud problem and reduced water usage.

The outdoor seating area, located off the great room, is protected by a canopy awning attached to a wood arbor. The light-colored paving stones on this and the dining patio are Arizona sandstone, and the dark borders are bluestone.

To help contain the lower terrace zones without introducing physical divisions, Van de Voorde suggested colorful patterned patios of Arizona sandstone and bluestone. She kept the original plants, using them to help define the two terraces and increase privacy on the sides of the yard adjacent to neighboring houses.

Used year-round, this easy-to-maintain outdoor room is a practical solution for a large family. According to Van de Voorde, the space works perfectly: the kids can enjoy their play, the adults can relax in the seating area and, when dinner is served, everyone can meet at the dining table.

FACING ABOVE: The fountain, made from granite with a bluestone rim and cap, visually anchors the seating section of the yard and brings the soothing sound of water to the entire space.

FACING BELOW: Food can be passed from the main kitchen to the outdoor kitchen through a sliding window. The refrigerator doors, warming drawer, grill cover and hood are stainless steel, and the patio is concrete stained to match the stone patios.

ABOVE: The outdoor dining room is on the same level as the seating area, but zones delineated by patios and synthetic turf form separations without the need for physical boundaries.

ECLECTIC OUTDOOR ROOM
Design: John Sofio, Built, Inc.
Photographs: Lone Pine Pictures

Challenge: Rework an underused patio into an outdoor space that reflects the owner's eclectic taste and provides a separate play area for kids.

Result: A functional outdoor room linked to the house with a glass conservatory, a playhouse for the children and a design that incorporates the owner's travel mementos.

Architect John Sofio took a break from modernism when he re-modeled this property in Laguna Nigel, California. The owner, a world traveler, wanted the new design to showcase the art and souvenirs she had collected during her trips to Africa and Europe, and in some places even build those memories right into the structure. She also asked for a more complete outdoor space and a special play area for her grandchildren.

Best described as eclectic, the house, located on a golf course two miles from the beach, now keeps the owner's travel memories close at hand. The interior walls, for example, are finished to resemble African mud huts, and the outdoor fireplace has been embedded with pieces of stones from her collection.

ABOVE: The steel and glass conservatory pops out of a wall of the existing house and extends into the garden.

FACING: The house is clad in cedar siding, a long-lasting choice for coastal climates. The walls and roof of the soaring conservatory are glass for a clear visual connection to the outdoor room beyond.

Sofio transformed an underused patio into a functional outdoor room complete with a built-in barbecue, a fireplace and dining area. The outdoor room, he says, feels like a natural extension of the house. "All that's missing is a roof over the patio," he points out.

This extension is accentuated with a glass conservatory attached to the patio side of the house. With its thin steel frame and glass roof and walls, the conservatory—really a glass room—serves as a sheer division between the interior rooms and the patio, emphasizing the interaction between the two spaces.

For the client's young grandchildren, Sofio took an existing playhouse on the site, gave it new paint and relocated it to a porch that overlooks the outdoor room. The playhouse is separate enough to allow the children their own space but close enough to the patio that the adults can easily monitor the kids' activity.

ABOVE: Repainted and relocated to a porch overlooking the outdoor room, the playhouse gives the owner's grandchildren their own separate play area while allowing the adults to monitor the kids' activity from the patio.

RIGHT: The functional outdoor room includes a built-in barbecue, a fireplace and a dining area. The fireplace has been embedded with stones from the owner's collection, and the stone patio floor is consistent with the organic theme of the remodeled spaces.

ELEGANT SCREENED PORCH

Design: Rick Harlan Schneider and Petros Zouzoulas, Inscape Studio
Photographs: Dan Redmond

Challenge: A well-ventilated and bug-proof outdoor room addition made from eco-friendly materials and designed to be both physically and visually separate from the main house.

Result: An airy pavilion-style screened porch set apart from the house and constructed of sustainably harvested cedar and environmentally sound framing lumber.

The owners of this Bethesda, Maryland, property are drawn to modern architecture but live in a Colonial-style house in a suburban neighborhood. Without having to resort to a remodel of their entire house, they were able to satisfy their contemporary cravings with a screened porch addition that is strikingly distinct from the main house.

Designed by architects Rick Harlan Schneider and Petros Zouzoulas of Inscape Studio, the 192-square-foot Butterfly Pavilion, so called because of its graceful butterfly roof structure and resemblance to an open-air beach pavilion, is a separate building accessed from the kitchen via a newly installed deck. The architects positioned the porch away from the house and treated it as an individual object for two reasons: to encourage the occupants to engage more fully with the rest of their property, and to protect the path of daylight that floods the kitchen, which might have been compromised had the porch been closer to the house. Keeping the structure separate also saved the owners money because the roof did not have to be tied into the existing house. Total design and construction costs came to about $50,000.

Schneider and Zouzoulas decided to place the building on piers, rather than pour a foundation, for greater flexibility. "The piers gave us the ability to site the structure in a way that didn't hit any major tree roots," Schneider explains. "On our first attempt, we found that a couple of the piers were near tree roots, so all we had to do was move the structure away from the roots."

LEFT: All four walls of the porch are screened to create cross ventilation, particularly important during the hot and humid summer months.

ABOVE: Carefully placed lighting beneath the canopy and around the perimeter of the building makes the porch an inviting place to spend an evening.

The building's "wrapping" responds directly to the immediate environment. On the sides that face the garage and a neighboring house, slats over the screens facilitate ventilation but are wide enough to ensure privacy. On the less-exposed yard side of the building, thin louvers instill a lightness and transparency in the structure and complement the delicacy of the roof, with its hovering steel frame canopy inset with acrylic fabric. The architects chose an eco-friendly variety of treated lumber for the framing and sustainably harvested cedar for the slats, louvers and deck.

The butterfly roof is also functional: heeding the owners' desire for a rain garden, the architects turned the V-shaped roof into a rain collector; a scupper on the roof funnels the water to a rain chain that terminates in the garden.

Sitting lightly on the ground, seemingly poised to take off, the Butterfly Pavilion is not only eye-catching, but a fresh and ecologically minded way to build an outdoor room.

ABOVE: The airy porch roof is reminiscent of a butterfly about to take flight, and the lightness of the structure is further enhanced by pier supports, used instead of a traditional foundation.

RIGHT: Slender louvers over the screens on the yard side of the porch ventilate the interior while helping to form an outdoor room that feels private. The steel frame roof structure is inset with an acrylic fabric canopy, a more eco-friendly material than vinyl. A scupper channels rainwater down a rain chain and into the garden.

LEFT: The pavilion's cedar siding and deck have been sealed with oil to prevent the wood from greying over time. The refreshment counter is also cedar covered with a clear-coat paint, and the custom bench, designed to fit the space, is not attached to the deck and thus can be moved around as desired. The deck leads to the kitchen for easy indoor/outdoor access.

ABOVE: Sustainably harvested cedar slats and louvers and arsenic-free Alkaline Copper Quaternary (ACQ)—treated framing lumber are the structure's primary materials. ACQ lumber is less toxic than traditional pressure-treated lumber, making it a greener choice.

MERGING OLD WITH NEW
Design: Ross Chapin, Ross Chapin Architects
Photographs: Ross Chapin

Challenge: Rework an old cabin into a family-oriented retreat with separate living zones linked to common gathering areas.

Result: A new house connected to the existing cabin by a warm and inviting outdoor room.

When the owners of a 1950s weekend cabin on Puget Sound's Whidbey Island decided to retire to the island, they soon realized that although the cabin exuded a rustic charm, it wasn't configured to accommodate their lifestyle or the frequent visits by their extended family.

Architect Ross Chapin suggested a clever and functional alternative to completely reworking the cabin: freshen it up with a light surface remodel and place a master suite right next to it. The couple now live comfortably in the 650-square-foot addition, while family members and friends stay in the cozy cabin next door. In this way, both the owners and their visitors have plenty of privacy. "The cabin needed so much repair that we would have had to redo the entire building," Chapin says. "I thought it was important not to destroy the innate character of the cabin, and this was the solution."

The final flourish was a covered outdoor living room in the space between the two structures, formed by a stone wall out of which projects

a substantial fireplace. The room is protected and warm, the perfect place to gather or simply sit and read a book. A dining patio extends from the room, and during inclement weather the table can be pulled into the covered area.

Chapin used cedar shingles on both buildings to visually and texturally connect them, and the cabin's original eaves were replaced with more dramatic extensions, giving its roof a greater sense of shelter. Other features include a cedar trellis, an elegant and airy ceiling structure inspired by a Japanese monastery temple the architect once visited, a skylight over the fireplace to bring natural light into the space and concrete patio pavers.

"The success of the project is in its simplicity and richness, and the way elements from the addition and the cabin are woven together," Chapin says. "The outdoor room allows the two buildings to function as a much larger unit, and the way they were joined together makes both houses feel one and the same."

ABOVE: The spruce ceiling is inset with a waterproof membrane, important in this rainy locale. The airiness of the ceiling structure was inspired by a Japanese temple once visited by the architect. The dining table can be moved into the protected space during wet weather.

FACING BELOW: The focal point of the outdoor room, the fireplace features local stone and small built-in ledges for displaying collectibles. A skylight above the fireplace sends sunlight into the space, and a round portal in the wall makes it possible to see people approaching the house. The double garden doors, made from salvaged red cedar, serve as the main entrance into the room from the driveway. The patio pavers are concrete.

LEFT: The addition (to the left) and the existing cabin (to the right) are connected with an outdoor room formed with a stone wall anchored by a stone fireplace. Both buildings are clad in durable cedar shingles, and the cabin was updated with larger eaves to enhance the sense of shelter. The end trellis, made from cedar, helps to visually weave the two forms together.

FOR KIDS ONLY

Design: John Sofio, Built, Inc.
Photographs: Lone Pine Pictures

Challenge: A structured play space for kids at a Los Angeles–area preschool.

Result: A bold take on the playhouse concept that pays homage to early California modernism.

I couldn't resist including this play structure by Los Angeles architect John Sofio. After all, don't kids deserve great outdoor rooms made just for them?

Designed for a nursery preschool in the famed Silverlake District of Los Angeles, this über-modern playhouse is scaled to size for young tots. Judging by the presence of such a structure, kids in this neighborhood are introduced at an early age to a bit of architectural history: early California modernist Richard Neutra built a house for himself in Silverlake and ran an office there.

"There's a real Neutra vibe going in this community because of his influences," Sofio says.

"The parents wanted the playhouse to reflect that sensibility. In this neighborhood, we teach them about modernism right from the beginning!"

Constructed with treated wood posts and metal studs and clad in sturdy Polygal polycarbonate sheeting, the playhouse has a metal roof and an observation platform with a view straight to Silverlake Reservoir. Its opposing walls slide open for a breezy indoor/outdoor connection, and a ramp allows the kids to ride their bikes right through the playhouse if so desired—without damaging the durable Trex decking. Window openings in the walls accommodate puppet shows, and ample shelving brings organization to dress-up and play time.

Now the burning question: Will these children grow up to build their own modern houses?

ABOVE: The primary materials on the playhouse are treated wood, metal, Polygal and durable Trex decking. The top deck is accessed by a small stair on the back of the structure.

FACING: The structure's opposing walls can slide open to create an indoor/outdoor space, and a ramp allows the kids to ride their bikes through the center of the playhouse. The window openings are used for puppet shows.

Indoor/Outdoor Connections

ADDRESSING SITE AND SOUND

Design: Michael Chacon and Maria Barmina
Photographs: Bernard André

Challenge: Create a comfortable, inviting outdoor space on an extremely narrow site in a neighborhood near a commuter railroad.

Result: A streamlined building with a private and quiet outdoor living space that follows from the rear great room.

The architects who designed this contemporary indoor/outdoor house in Palo Alto, California, literally took advantage of every inch of usable space. Thanks to their diligence, the streamlined building features a striking composition of forms and materials and a serene, protected backyard space that gives no hint of the busy neighborhood beyond.

Architects Michael Chacon and Maria Barmina were faced with numerous limitations from the onset of the design process. The lot, only forty feet wide by 150 feet deep, was further squeezed by six-foot setbacks on either side, reducing the maximum width of the house to a mere twenty-eight feet. Add to that the fact that the site is just 200 feet from a commuter railroad and adjacent to an expressway, and the obstacles to a serene outdoor space become evident.

FACING LEFT: The back patio connects to the great room through a multi-paneled glass door, and the upper deck is accessed by a staircase attached to the privacy wall, which features opaque portals that allow light to filter in without sacrificing privacy. The wall forms one side of the great room and continues out to the patio, making the two spaces appear to be one.

FACING RIGHT: Despite a narrow building site and other limitations, the house connects to its setting without overwhelming it. The façade reveals an elegant composition of shapes and textures, achieved with barrel vault roofs and stucco and red cedar as the dominant exterior materials.

ABOVE: The back of the house opens to the yard, which is protected on one side by a sixteen-foot-high concrete block privacy wall that is integral to the building. The wall buffers traffic noise and gives the outdoor space a feeling of enclosure.

"We had to figure out how to focus activities and design a welcoming and private outdoor environment in this noisy mixed-use neighborhood," Chacon explains.

The patio is shielded by a sixteen-foot-high concrete block privacy wall that also forms a wall of the great room. The wall reduces off-site noise and, with the help of an outdoor fireplace, "wraps" the patio in privacy without fully enclosing it. Opaque portals punched into the top of the wall send sunlight onto the patio.

Chacon describes the house as a precise example of what to do with limited space and an active setting. He adds, "Despite the many constraints, the result is spacious and clean. I see it as both an aesthetically pleasing and functional composition of spaces."

And when the train rolls by and sounds its horn, as it does several times an hour, the occupants of the house can sit outside, enjoy the day and pay little heed to the disruption.

FAR LEFT: The addition of a fireplace turned the patio into a true indoor/outdoor space. Designed to play off the clean lines of the house, the stucco-covered structure has only a stainless steel opening and no mantel or surround. The patio is covered in multicolored India slate tiles, an economical and beautiful material.

ABOVE: Light-colored bamboo flooring inside the great room contrasts with the darker slate outside, highlighting the transition between inside and out.

BOTTOM LEFT: An upper deck looks down over the backyard. For the deck, the architect chose ipe, a Brazilian hardwood that is a smart choice for outdoor spaces. The transparency of the railing allows for unimpeded views down into the yard.

TWO CONNECTED SPACES
Design: Michael Folonis, Michael W. Folonis and Associates
Photographs: Claudio Santini

Challenge: Turn the narrow space formed by an addition to an existing house into a private and comfortable outdoor room.

Result: A series of small patios that connect the two buildings, forming an outdoor living room and minimalist garden.

In bustling Santa Monica, California, the transition zone between an existing house and a new addition has been transformed into a peaceful outdoor room with connections to the interiors of both structures.

When architect Michael Folonis was asked to design a soundproof practice room and recording studio for his client, a professional musician, he decided that the most workable solution would be to add a separate building next to the main house, which he also designed. The addition contains a basement recording studio, a garage and an upper-level apartment/office in a compact 1,100 square feet. Once construction was completed, Folonis discovered an unexpected opportunity for an outdoor living room in the twelve-foot-wide strip of land between the two buildings.

"We have many opportunities here for indoor/outdoor spaces, thanks to the climate," Folonis says. "In this case, a natural link between two structures was, with little impact, turned into an easily accessed outdoor room."

ABOVE: The 1,100-square-foot addition houses a basement recording studio, garage and an upper-level apartment/office. The primary exterior materials on this and the main house are smooth steel trowel finish stucco colored with a white pigment in some areas and left uncolored in others, stacked bond concrete block and mahogany. The outdoor room is sheltered from the street by a concrete block wall.

FACING: The addition is connected to the main house by a series of small patios, the largest of which forms an outdoor living room.

To accommodate the level change from the house to the addition, Folonis installed a series of stepped-down patios accented by minimalist landscaping that doesn't intrude into the usable space. A low-profile steel stair, attached to the side of the addition to maximize the patio area, leads up to the apartment, and the garage is just a few steps down from the central patio.

This resourceful configuration of patios and side and rooftop decks gives the owner a variety of options for experiencing the neighborhood. Depending on his mood, he can choose privacy on the sheltered patio or head up to one of the more open decks.

The exterior materials, including stucco, cement block and mahogany, are a suitable backdrop for this peaceful outdoor environment. "This is a quiet and calming place to be, even in the midst of a busy neighborhood," Folonis says.

FACING LEFT: River stones and ornamental grasses bring subtle texture to the patio.

FACING RIGHT: Although only twelve feet wide and thirty-five feet deep, the space between the two buildings easily accommodates an outdoor living room. A wood fence at the property line helps enclose the patio for greater privacy.

ABOVE: The concrete patio complements the minimalist landscaping and modern furnishings.

LEFT: The low-maintenance garden features an artistic arrangement of river stones, ornamental grasses and simple concrete pavers.

LOFT-STYLE DESERT BEAUTY

Design: Aldo Andreoli, Sanba International
Photographs: Marco Ricca and Blacky's Studio

Challenge: An indoor/outdoor house that adjusts to the climatic fluctuations of its desert setting and responds texturally to the surroundings.

Result: A flexible design that keeps the house cool in the summer and warm in the winter, and which integrates with the landscape through the use of natural materials.

The backdrop is undeniably stunning: the regal red rock formations and pinion and juniper forests of Sedona, Arizona. Natural beauty aside, however, the region presents an intriguing challenge for an indoor/outdoor house: for six months of the year, it can be hot enough for air-conditioning, while during the other six months heat is often necessary.

Owned and designed by architect Aldo Andreoli, the house responds to the sometimes hot, sometimes cold weather with a site orientation and floor plan that capture low-angle winter sunlight to warm the interiors and circulate cooling breezes through the rooms during the summer. Influenced by the Italian-born Andreoli's seventeen years in New York City, where he remodeled a number of lofts, the loft-like house contains the main living spaces within a simple rectangle capped with a barrel vault roof. Inside, the soaring ceiling structure, supported by a series of glulam beams, gives the house what Andreoli describes as a "shrine-like" feel. Indeed, this introspective quality was important to the architect, who moved to Sedona

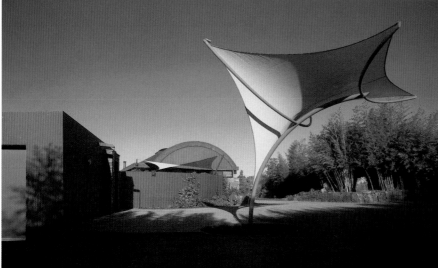

FACING: The entry is marked by a free-standing shade canopy that can be moved and rotated to accommodate the angle of the sun at different times of the year. The exterior stucco is similar in color to Sedona's red rock formations. Photo by Blacky's Studio.

ABOVE: The loft-like building is essentially a rectangle capped with a barrel vault roof clad in copper. A curved privacy wall partially encloses the master bedroom patio, forming a secluded place to take in the gardens and scenery. Photo by Marco Ricca.

LEFT: The lines of the wedge-shaped negative-edge pool correspond to the barrel vault roof. The louver extends beyond the house on either side, shading the building and adjacent outdoor spaces. Photo by Marco Ricca.

ABOVE: The house features materials that harmonize with the landscape, including copper, cedar and Arizona flagstone. Photo by Marco Ricca.

RIGHT: An operable louver system, made from cedar and supported by steel columns, can be closed to shade the lower-level interiors during the summer and opened to welcome lower-angle winter sunlight. Sliding glass doors circulate cooling breezes through the rooms, particularly important when the mercury rises. The outdoor shower at the far end of the louver is clad in blue mosaic tiles. Photo by Marco Ricca.

BELOW RIGHT: Sliding glass doors create a clear indoor/outdoor interaction between the yoga room and pool patio. The interior floors are jarrah wood and the patio is flagstone. The negative-edge pool reaches out to the high desert setting. Photo by Marco Ricca.

seeking quietude after hectic city life. He even created a special yoga room that opens onto the pool/Jacuzzi patio through sliding glass doors and overlooks the sweeping high-desert vista.

The architect wanted the house to integrate with the landscape, both in style and materiality. The building steps down into the site, forming a second level at the pool side of the property. He chose materials that are visually and texturally compatible with the reds and greens of the desert, including copper roofing, which ages into a green patina, and Arizona flagstone, which is similar in color to the surrounding red rock.

The home's indoor/outdoor connections are expressed in a variety of ways, most notably in large windows and sliding glass doors that join the interiors to the gardens and pool area. The master bedroom extends out onto a walled patio that is a private place to relax and experience the gardens and scenery. One of the home's most impressive features is an operable louver system that gracefully meets the demands of the seasons: the louvers can be opened to permit sunlight into the house during the winter or closed to help cool the building during the summer. The outdoor spaces are inviting with an outdoor shower clad in brilliant blue tiles, a wedge-shaped negative-edge pool that seems to merge with the horizon and a Jacuzzi spa.

The drama of the ceiling structure is emphasized at night. Photo by Marco Ricca.

HOUSE WITH TWO PERSONALITIES

Design: Ron Godfredsen and Danna Sigal, Godfredsen Sigal Architects

Photographs: Claudio Santini

Challenge: A backyard pool and patio with a seamless connection to the house, and an architectural style that doesn't overwhelm the unassuming neighborhood.

Result: A house with a "split" personality: a minimal, one-story design that is low and private on the street side but rises exuberantly at the back of the property, connecting the house to the site with a distinctive indoor/outdoor space.

This house in Mar Vista, California, has two personalities, an intentional strategy employed by architects Ron Godfredsen and Danna Sigal to create a house that would fit into its neighborhood and feature a dynamic indoor/outdoor connection.

After studying the quiet suburb, which is populated mostly by tract homes, the architects arrived at a design with a subdued street façade

and, at the back, an undeniably high-spirited embrace of the setting.

"The clients didn't want a house that would be too showy from the street, but at the same time they wanted the back of the house to relate to the natural environment," Godfredsen explains. "In this case, all the drama takes place at the back of house."

The low-slung façade of the 2,400-square-foot house rises at the

FACING: The scaled-back front landscaping is defined by discrete areas of color.

LEFT: The interplay of the home's two roofs is visible in the backyard. The more flamboyant counterpart to the understated façade, the side of the house is paralleled by a pool set closer than normal to the building to heighten the interaction between the interior and exterior spaces. The solidity of the outdoor fireplace anchors the soaring top canopy, which shades the patio. A scupper at the edge of the lower roof funnels rainwater into the yard.

ABOVE: The great room "glass box" is supported by a steel colonnade that breaks up the expanse of glass and helps reduce the scale of the building. Carex, an ornamental grass, creates the look of a meadow.

FACING: The proximity of the house and pool intensifies the effect of a continuous indoor/outdoor space. Butt-joint glazing on the floor-to-ceiling box further blurs the line between inside and out and offers an unimpeded view of the pool and yard.

The webbed steel support columns have been inset with strips of Douglas fir to match the windows.

back with a soaring roof structure and opens to the yard with a glass box that parallels the great room and rises in line with the upper roof. This glass wall is supported by a colonnade of steel columns whose webs have been filled in with strips of Douglas fir to match the windows. Round steel columns support the top canopy, which shades an outdoor sitting area focused on a fireplace clad in charcoal-grey stucco to match the front of the house. The proximity of the pool to the house amplifies the relationship between the indoor and outdoor spaces: light from the pool bounces onto the interior walls, blurring the line between where the water ends and the house begins.

The overall effect is one of transparency, which makes it possible to engage with the outdoors from a variety of points within the house. As Godfredsen puts it, "The house is relentless about making you look outside."

FACING: Another indoor/outdoor connection can be found in the master bathroom, which opens to a private courtyard. The tub is clad in German greenstone and the wall is limestone. A sheet of laminated glass encloses the shower.

ABOVE: Large Douglas fir awning windows circulate fresh air through the interiors. The outdoor fireplace, visible through the window, is clad in stucco to match the front exterior and features a stainless steel surround.

MALIBU FIXER-UPPER

Design: Toni Lewis and Marc Schoeplein, Lewis Schoeplein Architects
Photographs: Claudio Santini

Challenge: Turn a cramped floor plan into a series of free-flowing spaces that connect gracefully to the backyard and offer flexibility for an active young family.

Result: A budget-conscious remodel that has freed the home of its claustrophobic plan and dated materiality, and features clear interactions between the indoors and outdoors.

Sometimes, bringing a home in tune with its surroundings requires changing the house itself. Such was the case with this home, located on a Malibu, California, hillside overlooking the Pacific Ocean. With its small windows, dated materials and awkward transitions to the spacious but underused backyard, the house needed a new look and attitude.

Built in the 1960s, the 2,300-square-foot house still had the shag carpet and spray-on ceiling popular at the time, and an equally problematic floor plan of boxy walled-in rooms whose undersized windows didn't even begin to capture the natural beauty of the setting. Aware of its innate potential, architects Toni Lewis and Marc Schoeplein designed a remodel to reconfigure the house into a flexible and family-oriented indoor/outdoor dwelling. "The house had what

we describe in this business as good bones, meaning its structure was very sound," Lewis explains. "There were a lot of good elements in the building to work with, we just needed to open up the rooms and allow them to breathe."

Malibu's strict rules regarding adding on to existing structures prompted the architects to take the path of least resistance: instead of altering the foundation, they worked with the original footprint, thereby avoiding the lengthy approvals process. The roof structure was also left intact, and instead of moving the windows, they simply enlarged the openings. Inside, walls were knocked down to form an open floor plan.

The interiors are now connected to the backyard with sliding glass doors at the dining and family room areas. A deck adjacent to the dining room is protected by a

trellis-like overhang and broad support columns, giving it the feel of an outdoor room. The focal point of the backyard is a kidney-shaped pool, located off the family room.

"Although this was basically just an interior remodel with an exterior facelift, the house has been transformed," Lewis says. "There are very few divisions between the indoor and outdoor spaces."

ABOVE: The 1960s house was given an exterior facelift with a fresh coat of stucco, larger windows and a new front door that pivots open to send ocean breezes through the interiors.

FACING: The revised interiors have been freed from the choppy original floor plan and visually and physically connected to the outdoors with larger windows and sliding glass doors.

FACING: The kidney-shaped pool is surrounded by a spacious concrete patio and accessed through sliding glass doors.

ABOVE LEFT: The soft colors of the home's yellow-green stucco, Douglas fir (sliding door) and plantation-grown mahogany (decking) harmonize with the natural landscape.

BELOW LEFT: The trellis-like deck covering is painted Douglas fir inset with translucent Polygal panels, an insulating material originally designed for greenhouses but also popular for residential applications. The Polygal lets light onto the deck and protects it from rain.

ABOVE RIGHT: A Douglas fir sliding door replaced a small window in the dining area and, when open, joins the room to an adjacent deck. The lines of the interior rafters were continued on the deck's trellis-like covering, furthering the visual effect of an indoor/outdoor space. The sliding door brought another benefit: the owners' young children can run freely in and out of the house without having to open and close a door.

A NEW VIEW
Design: Mark English, Mark English Architects
Photographs: Michael O'Callahan

Challenge: A steep drop on the site, a close-in neighborhood, and finding an unobtrusive way to capture the dramatic views of the San Francisco skyline.

Result: An indoor/outdoor space that provides privacy and views and that took advantage of an existing building on the site to support a kitchen addition and adjacent deck.

Although this home sits high on a hill and has a clear view of downtown San Francisco, in its original form it didn't fully capture the impact of those views. After studying the site, architect Mark English proposed an elegant solution: a curving kitchen addition oriented to perfectly frame the skyline and an adjacent deck supported by an existing structure.

"Before the addition of the deck, the back of the house ended abruptly," English explains. "There were no inviting views, nor was there an outdoor living space. In this case, the view was the greatest asset we had."

Before embarking on design and construction, English scrutinized the site's weather patterns, determining that the city's famous bank of fog often stops about 300 feet short of the house. When the fog does blow over the house, the deck, which is mid-level to the main structure, is protected from the elements.

The curved addition opens to the deck via French doors and is positioned to lead the eye straight toward the skyline. Responding to the owner's cues for a minimalist outdoor space, English kept the deck free of built-in seating, eating areas and other outdoor features. This allows the owner to be flexible with the space, pulling tables and chairs outside for a gathering or placing a single chair for a quiet place to read. The rail is solid on one side to provide a sense of security against a steep twenty-five-foot plunge to a neighboring garden, and transparent on the other two sides for unimpeded views to the courtyard below. The addition roof is covered with a pebble garden reminiscent of a Japanese garden. English did not put a top guard rail on the addition, opting instead for an almost spare look. However, brass arbors on the top and bottom edges of the building will eventually support foliage

which, when grown in, will soften the façade.

"One of my main goals was to create a peaceful presentation," the architect says. "We didn't want a lot going on, just a simple connection between the interior and exterior spaces."

ABOVE: A pebble garden on the addition roof serves as a delicate contrast to the rougher cobble stones of the courtyard below. From this angle, the curve and view-capturing orientation of the addition and its 300-square-foot deck are visible.

FACING: Brass arbors on the top and bottom edges of the addition will eventually support foliage, providing shade and softening the façade.

FAR LEFT: A separate building on the site was shored up with a new foundation and fresh siding and then turned into a platform for the deck. The addition's "skin" is copper, and the guard rail is made from painted steel. A breezeway below leads from the courtyard to an outdoor stair, which in turn leads to a formal dining room.

ABOVE: Tall windows and a skylight bring light into the addition. French doors open to the deck, and the polished limestone floors give way to slate and cherry outside.

LEFT: Brazilian cherry decking matches the butcher block on the kitchen island, and Chinese jade-green slate lends a subtle color to the minimalist exterior space. The solid portion of the rail, designed to conceal a twenty-five-foot drop to the ground, is made from hammered copper sheet metal glued to cement board panels and topped with a guardrail sheathed in copper. The planters are cast concrete.

LAKE HOUSE ON A BUDGET
Design: Daniel Johnson, Design-Build-Studio
Photographs: Carolyn Bates

Challenge: A budget-minded house able to accommodate large gatherings and provide a feeling of connection to the outdoors during all seasons.

Result: A flexible floor plan with well-defined public and private areas, and a spacious screened porch and dining room that both open to the setting.

The owners of this rural New Hampshire retreat wanted a weekend house that would accommodate family gatherings and feature year-round indoor/outdoor spaces. They also had a tight budget and wanted to use recycled and salvaged materials wherever possible.

Designed by architect Daniel Johnson, the house rests lightly on the land and is sited for maximum solar gain and protection from the elements. The floor plan, a series of well-defined but flexible public and private zones, includes a large screened porch that projects into the landscape. To further accentuate the building's indoor/outdoor relationships, Johnson installed an insulated glass garage door at the dining room; the door can be lifted to fully open the room to the outdoors.

The site, which is flanked by a river and lake frontage, already had a garage on it. Johnson preserved the existing foundation and then incorporated it into the new building, a move that minimized additional site work and saved trees that otherwise might have been disturbed. "The site remains a forest with a small house embedded

FACING: The foundation from an existing building on the site was preserved and expanded, allowing the house to be placed into the setting without disrupting the trees. The simple roof form effectively sheds snow and has large overhangs to help protect the building from the area's sometimes harsh weather. The house is clad in affordable cement board siding.

LEFT: The screened porch is an inviting place to gather in the evenings. Placing the porch on piers rather than a foundation minimized additional site work, lowering the overall impact of construction and preserving nearby trees.

within it," the architect points out.

The local climate, characterized by prevailing winds that sweep in off the lake, dictated a building that could shield itself from the elements. "The climate there is tough—there's a lot of wind, rain and snow," Johnson explains. "Although the best views face north toward the lake, the wind comes from that direction. This is pleasant in the summer but harsh in the winter, so we had to address that."

Johnson's design ventilates the house during the summer and defends it against frigid winter air. A shed roof slopes lower to the ground on the north side of the site, acting as a wind buffer for the living room and the adjacent screened porch. To the south, the roof rises dramatically, culminating in a double-height porch ceiling. Large roof overhangs offer additional protection from the weather, and a fireplace heats the porch during cooler days and nights.

The budget was kept in check with a variety of recycled and reclaimed materials including glass bathroom tiles and structural steel elements. Low-cost and low-maintenance materials include off-the-shelf trusses, industrial metal roofing, cement board siding and engineered lumber.

Johnson describes the home's indoor/outdoor areas as "interconnected and overlapped, with each enhancing the other and making the spaces seem larger than they are."

ABOVE: The dining room opens to the outdoors with an insulated glass garage door that slides up and is disguised inside by a plywood panel hanging from the ceiling. The interior flooring is local maple.

RIGHT: Full-height screens on the porch filter sunlight and bring the space into close contact with the trees.

LEFT: A double-sided fireplace merges the porch and living room, and in cold weather the porch can be closed off from the interiors with a glass door. The connection between the spaces is emphasized with a concrete threshold. The dark portion of the porch floor is recycled plastic GeoDeck. The photographer's dog, Lady Dickens, seems quite comfortable.

ABOVE: The double-height screened porch juts out from the building like the prow of a ship, extending the space directly into the treed site.

BEDROOM THAT OPENS TO THE OUTDOORS

Design: Joshua Coggeshall,
Cog Work Shop

Photographs: Claudio Santini and
Deborah Bird

Challenge: A strict budget and a request for a bedroom addition with a dramatic connection to the setting.

Result: A low-cost but architecturally compelling bedroom "box" with a wall that opens fully to the garden.

The owners of this Venice, California, house wanted a low-cost bedroom addition that would make a memorable indoor/outdoor statement and take advantage of the mild climate. When architect Joshua Coggeshall presented a design that linked the new room to the yard through French doors, the owners decided to go even further.

"They said, 'Wouldn't it be great if the whole wall could disappear?'" Coggeshall recalls. "They liked the idea of being able to open up an entire section of their home, rather than just a door. That's when things started to get exciting."

With the budget firmly in mind, Coggeshall designed a west-facing bedroom "box" that captures the ocean breezes and looks out onto the garden and an adjacent art studio. The room opens completely to the yard with a 300-pound garage-like door that lifts with a system of ropes, pulleys and cleats. When the door is raised, the space flows out onto the deck and interacts with the lush landscaping. When the door is lowered, it disappears into the architecture, forming an eye-catching exterior detail.

The addition is constructed entirely of wood, with different "skins" joined together with what the architect describes as "ease and order." To save money and add visual interest to the structure, Coggeshall chose to expose parts of the building rather than cover them. "Attaching the skins was an act of celebrating, exposing and revealing all the connections," he points out. "Instead of treating the addition like small architecture, we treated it like large furniture, with precise connections between the various materials."

ABOVE: The 800-square-foot house is just ten blocks from the beach but in its original form had no direct outdoor access. Photo by Claudio Santini.

FACING: Care was taken during construction not to disturb a large banana tree in the yard. The exterior of the wood structure is clad in "raw" cement board siding attached with stainless steel fasteners. Opening the door exposes the entire room to the garden. Photo by Claudio Santini.

ABOVE LEFT: The porch of an adjacent art studio faces the back of the main house, enhancing the connection between the two buildings. Photo by Claudio Santini.

ABOVE RIGHT: Although it weighs nearly 300 pounds, the door lifts easily, thanks to an unobtrusive pulley system. The overhang, designed to shade the deck and bedroom, was constructed with redwood slats set into a Douglas fir frame. Translucent Polygal panels in the door allow sunlight into the room and provide adequate insulation during the comparatively chilly winter months. The low-cost railing is strung with galvanized wire. Photo by Claudio Santini.

BELOW: The bedroom provides both an outdoor experience and the comfort of a traditional room. A side door, visible on the right wall of the addition, can be used to access the bedroom when the main door is closed. Photo by Deborah Bird.

FACING: The addition's four main materials were chosen for their affordability and durability: cement board siding, birch plywood, translucent Polygal door panels and drywall. The weather-resistant redwood deck has extra-long steps that double as seating during parties. Photo by Claudio Santini.

Materials had to be inexpensive and able to withstand the weathering effects of the coastal environment. Coggeshall decided on four primary materials, all of which are durable and affordable: cement board siding, birch plywood, drywall and translucent Polygal, a greenhouse material with excellent UV-protection and insulation properties. The box itself is clad in "raw" cement board siding attached with stainless steel fasteners. Polygal panels inset into the door allow natural light into the room while keeping it private when the door is down. When the door is up, sunlight bounces off the panels and onto the walls, which are "wrapped" in birch plywood. The bedroom and deck are shaded with a simple overhang made from redwood and Douglas fir.

Despite cost restraints, the addition makes an architectural statement and is successful in its key purpose: a flexible indoor/outdoor connection.

"I like working with budgets," Coggeshall says. "It's fun to push the boundaries of materials and find ways to make them more interesting."

ESCAPE FROM THE TEXAS HEAT
Design: Mark English, Mark English Architects
Photographs: Star Jennings

Challenge: Create outdoor spaces that are cool and inviting, even during hot summer days, and place the house into its setting without disrupting the landscape.

Result: Front and back outdoor living spaces that are shaded by trees and protected from the elements by exaggerated roof overhangs, and a simple, straightforward materiality that doesn't overpower the site.

When he set out to design this Austin house, architect Mark English clearly understood his primary task: create a home with outdoor living areas that can be used year-round, even during the intense heat of the Texas summer.

Prior to construction, English took a model of the house to the site and used it to track the path of the sun, a process that revealed which sections of the building would require the most shading and protection. His strategy for making the outdoor spaces usable in all kinds of weather was twofold: a terraced back patio shaded and protected from rain by generous roof overhangs, and a front courtyard entrance and gathering space tucked into a stand of existing oaks. (So important were the trees to the shading of the house that English made sure none of them were removed during excavation.) Thanks to this thoughtful planning, the home is pleasingly flexible: the owners have the option of gathering in the courtyard or on the patio, or both, depending on the temperature and time of day.

The house, inspired by the Tuscan farmhouses English encountered during his studies in Italy, is composed of three sections linked together with glass panes in a compound-like arrangement. The heart of the house is a barrel-vaulted great room that opens to a spacious patio complete with a firepit. To mark the boundary between the house and an adjacent golf course, just steps

FACING: A low stone wall in the front courtyard can serve as a seating bench during gatherings. To protect the trellis from water and termite damage, the architect placed the columns on galvanized metal stand-offs that keep them off the ground.

ABOVE: The architect preserved the existing oaks by placing the house carefully on the site. The trees shade the front courtyard entrance, which the owners use as a year-round entertainment and gathering space. The house features sand-finished stucco painted a soft green.

away, English raised the back patio onto a three-foot-high plinth. "In this development, it was important to have a sense of separation between public and private spaces," he explains. "That we were able to achieve this without installing a deck railing means the house can connect more directly to its surroundings."

Local design guidelines were met with a pared-down exterior palette of salvaged Douglas fir, blown down in a storm in New Mexico and trucked to Texas, sandstone and light green stucco. The overall effect is of a building that looks right at home in its setting—and inviting on a scorching day.

FACING: A breezeway between the garage and main section of the house serves as a covered transition to the home's outdoor spaces. The walls are sandstone and the paving stones are quartzite which, with its subtle glitter, contrasts nicely with the sandstone.

ABOVE LEFT: The expansive great room, with its dramatic barrel vault roof clad in zinc, opens directly to the back patio through French doors. The patio is raised onto a three-foot plinth to visually separate the home from the adjacent golf course. Generous roof overhangs, supported by Douglas fir columns to match the front trellis, shade the patio, making it usable year-round and cool even during the hottest months of the year. The eaves also protect the house from rain.

ABOVE RIGHT: Salvaged Douglas fir was used for the front trellis and oiled to deepen its color. The trellis serves as both a functional (plants can be grown over it for more shade) and aesthetic complement to the façade, clad in local sandstone. The windows are painted wood.

LEFT: A firepit makes the patio a congenial place to gather. Broad steps double as seating.

OUTDOOR CONNECTIONS FROM EVERY ROOM

Design: Michael Folonis,
Michael W. Folonis and Associates
Photographs: Claudio Santini

Challenge: A narrow, sloping lot on a busy corner and the request for a small house with dramatic indoor/outdoor connections.

Result: A house that wraps around a private courtyard and engages with the outdoors from every room.

The owners of this modest one-bedroom house, located just six blocks from the Pacific Ocean in Santa Monica, California, are originally from Wisconsin, where year-round indoor/outdoor living presents obvious climatic challenges.

When the couple decided to retire to California, they hired architect Michael Folonis to design a small, low-maintenance house that would frame a view from every window and present opportunities for outdoor connections at every corner. Aside from these initial challenges, Folonis also had to contend with a narrow, sloping site and a busy corner location.

Folonis responded with a streamlined 1,300-square-foot building organized into three sections: a carport, guest room and bath on the lowest part of the slope, followed by an art gallery, patio and garden in the center of the building, and a kitchen, living room, bedroom and bathroom on the highest part of the site. The

FACING: The house turns its back on the busy street, wrapping around a private courtyard on the less-exposed side of the property. The primary exterior materials are a combination of charcoal-grey concrete block and uncolored smooth steel trowel finish stucco.

LEFT: Every room in the house has a direct indoor/outdoor relationship. The living room patio is raised above the courtyard and accessed through sliding glass doors that complement the gallery doors. The ample glass on the house encourages passive solar heating, and the sliding doors ventilate the interiors.

TOP: Pulling back the glass doors expands the gallery, just ten feet wide and designed as the transition zone between the lower entry and upper living areas. The concrete patio pavers intentionally match the interior concrete floors, for the visual effect of a continuous indoor/outdoor space.

ABOVE: The transparent qualities of the house are even more pronounced in this view from the kitchen to the art gallery.

RIGHT: A wide expanse of glass fronts the art gallery, and sliding glass doors can be pulled back to join the room to the courtyard. A steel trellis, attached to the extended roof overhang, helps screen the gallery from sunlight.

sections progress up the slope in two-step increments, and the house as a whole turns its back on the street, wrapping around an inner courtyard on the less-exposed side of the property.

Clear physical connections to the outdoors can be found in every interior space of the house. The central art gallery opens completely to the courtyard and garden through large sliding glass doors, fostering a lightness and transparency that are under-scored with a delicate steel trellis attached to the roof overhang.

For the exterior, Folonis chose simple materials with a focus on uncolored smooth trowel finish stucco, concrete block and expanses of glass to enhance the building's passive solar properties. The concrete absorbs heat, the windows welcome sunlight and the sliding doors ventilate the interiors.

"The theme of this house is transparency," Folonis says. "The configuration of articulated spaces, each of which embraces the outdoor environment, in many ways makes indoor and outdoor living one and the same."

Water

SOPHISTICATION IN A SMALL YARD

Design: Trevor Abramson, Abramson Teiger Architects
Photographs: John Linden

Challenge: Turn a small backyard into a place to gather and unwind after a busy day, with easy indoor/outdoor access.

Result: A pool/Jacuzzi that extends from an elegantly appointed covered sitting area, and large glass doors on the garden-facing rooms.

For his own West Los Angeles house, architect Trevor Abramson wanted an outdoor room for relaxing and throwing parties that would relate to the architecture of the home and, above all, not overpower the small backyard.

The architect achieved his goal with a covered outdoor sitting room and adjacent pool/Jacuzzi that together reveal what can be accomplished even when the yard is limited in size. The sitting room is located just off the kitchen and features a concrete floor that extends from inside, for a seamless indoor/outdoor transition. The pool then follows from the sitting area. Together, the house, patio and pool are cohesive in their design and display an understated sophistication.

Conscious of the importance of privacy, Abramson "closed" the street-facing side of the house, downsizing the windows and using sandblasted glass to allow light inside. The back of the house, however, stands in sharp contrast to the front: there, large

FACING: The street side of the house is deliberately quiet in its design while the back opens to the yard. The main exterior materials are white stucco and vertical grain Douglas fir. Panels of sandblasted glass allow natural light inside without affecting privacy.

LEFT: Working creatively with limited space, the architect revamped the yard into a combined outdoor sitting room and pool/Jacuzzi. The house provides easy access to the yard through wide sliding glass doors at the living and dining areas and a bifold glass door at the kitchen that opens to the covered patio. One side of the pool is delicately curved, tempering the strong horizontal and vertical lines of the house.

FAR LEFT: The roof of the outdoor sitting room is formed by the second-story master bedroom patio. To further enhance the indoor/outdoor feel of the yard, the architect continued the concrete floors of the kitchen out onto the patio. The ceiling joists are redwood and the support column is clad in smooth steel trowel plaster.

LEFT: The outdoor sitting room looks out onto the pool and its accompanying Jacuzzi, which is positioned at the far end of the property and partially enclosed with a smooth steel trowel plaster wall. The architect intentionally placed the Jacuzzi away from the house for a more private, secluded experience.

Mondrian-esque windows frame views of the yard. The second-story master bedroom also reaches out to the yard with a spacious patio that overlooks the pool and forms the roof of the outdoor sitting area. Bifold glass doors at the kitchen and sliding glass doors at the dining and living rooms make it possible to enter the yard from a variety of points within the house.

The pool itself is a work of art, delicately curved on one side and terminating in a Jacuzzi partially enclosed by a plaster wall. The pool tiles are a combination of two shades of light blue that impart a shimmering quality to the water, an effect that is even more dramatic at night.

"I envisioned the house and backyard as one continuous space," Abramson says. "We have the doors open all the time, and the yard is great for parties. People can move easily between the inside and outside and, because it's not too big, there is a closer, more intimate interaction."

The home's Mondrian-esque window pattern is even more dramatic at night, as is the shimmer of the light blue pool tiles.

MODERN WATER-FOCUSED MASTERPIECE

Design: Aldo Andreoli,
Sanba International
Photographs: Blacky's Studio

Challenge: Incorporate water into a desert site in a manner that responds to the style of the architecture.

Result: A sweeping negative-edge pool that follows the contours of the house and acts as a visual and physical extension of the interiors.

This modern house and its accompanying pool are every bit as eye-catching as their beautiful setting. Designed by architect Aldo Andreoli, the house, located in the red-rock paradise of Sedona, Arizona, looks like a piece of art dropped right into the desert. Perhaps the home's most striking feature is an eighty-five-foot-long negative-edge swimming pool that sweeps along the façade, reflecting the image of the building on its surface.

The main living areas and outdoor spaces are oriented toward the north to minimize solar gain during the hot summers and optimize privacy and views. Andreoli aimed for a close dialogue between inside and out, one that in this example evolved out of the prominent water elements that set the architectural tone of the property. In addition to the pool, there is a Jacuzzi off the master bedroom and, in the house, an inner courtyard complete with a small pond.

FACING: The house is nestled among the red rocks and juniper- and pinion-dotted landscape of Sedona and features exterior materials that blend with the natural setting, including copper fascia and stucco in a warm terra-cotta color.

LEFT: The pool side of the house is a glass wall inset with sliding doors that offer direct access to the patio.

The pool side of the house embraces the outdoors with a wall of glass inset with sliding doors that open onto a partially covered patio that runs parallel to the structure. The pool forms the next layer of the multi-tiered yard, which progresses down into a cultivated garden. The outdoor spaces follow the natural contours of the terrain and, although they are connected, have enough implied separation for privacy.

Andreoli prefers to use materials that complement the landscape, and for this house he chose stucco in a terra-cotta color similar to the surrounding red rock and copper fascia that corresponds to the pinion and juniper forests. Flagstone patios and sand-colored decking round out the palette.

"There is a constant dialogue between the interiors and the water outside," the architect says. "You can be in the living room and clearly see the pool, which is very much part of the house, not just an addition to it. This house is all about water."

FACING: The roof overhang is supported by substantial glulam beams left exposed and held in place at their bases with metal plates.

LEFT: The pool gradually widens as it moves away from the master bedroom. The outdoor spaces are arranged in easy-to-access layers designed for separation and privacy and to accommodate the natural contours of the site.

ABOVE: A stucco-clad masonry wall divides the main patio and lower deck. Accessible from both ends of the pool, the lower deck is covered in durable and low-maintenance Trex decking.

FACING: A sitting area off the guest section of the house gives visitors a quiet place to relax and enjoy the scenery.

LEFT: Located off the master bedroom at one end of the pool, the Jacuzzi is clad in flagstone to match the patio.

BELOW: Reflected on the surface of the pool, the house appears to double in height. The close relationship between the house and pool is apparent in this intentional visual effect.

PRIVATE OUTDOOR SPA
Design: Matt Charlot
Photographs: Marcus Hanschen and Matt Charlot

Challenge: Revamp an underused backyard into a private outdoor spa shielded from the neighbors.

Result: A two-level deck enclosed with a wood lattice that forms a sun-filled space featuring a hot tub, outdoor shower and built-in seating.

The sloping backyard of this Bay Area house has been transformed into a spa retreat with a two-level deck equipped with a hot tub, outdoor shower and plenty of comfortable seating. The transformation is all the more dramatic when you consider how the yard looked before the remodel. Filled with weeds and devoid of character, it was uninviting, too exposed to neighboring houses and lacking in creature comforts.

Landscape designer Matt Charlot helped the owners bring to life their vision for a private outdoor spa attached to the back of their house and a yard that would better accommodate their young children. The result is a deck arranged in two connected levels and "wrapped" in lattice panels that enclose the space without blocking sunlight. In some areas the leaves of trees even poke through the square openings in the lattice, making the connection between the deck and the yard even more pronounced. The predominant material is redwood, chosen for

its innate resistance to termites and weather and used for the lattices, flooring, built-in seating and a trellis that rings the top of the deck and in time will be covered with vines. Retaining walls terraced below the deck organize the sloping yard and form a play area for the couple's children.

Connected by a wide step, the two levels give the owners a great deal of flexibility with how they use the space. The upper deck, with its perimeter seating, coffee table and barbecue, is perfect for gatherings, while the lower deck, with its built-in hot tub and outdoor shower, is intended for relaxation and rejuvenation.

Although self-contained, the deck maintains a relationship to the rest of the yard. "There is a great feeling of privacy when you're inside the deck, but it's not so closed off that the outdoor environment is forgotten," Charlot says.

And homeowners take note: the stair from the deck to the yard captures views of downtown Oakland

that weren't visible before the remodel. The owners can stand on the landing and see for miles, happy that they not only have a serene and functional outdoor room, but one that raised the value of their property.

seamed to prevent rainwater from pooling on their surfaces. The backs of the benches are angled for comfort and, for design consistency, repeat the lattice wall pattern. Photo by Matt Charlot.

FAR LEFT: The upper deck is large enough for entertaining but intimate in scale. The decking, lattice and trellis are all redwood. The lattices enclose the space without blocking sunlight and the perimeter trellis will eventually support plants. Photo by Matt Charlot.

FACING ABOVE: The two-level deck attaches to the back of the house, forming a private outdoor spa and living area. The landing of the deck stair, which leads down into the yard, is high enough to capture views of downtown Oakland. Photo by Marcus Hanschen.

FACING BELOW: The seats of the built-in redwood benches are cupped for comfort and

ABOVE: Separated from the upper deck with a single step, the lower deck features a hot tub and planters with the same lattice pattern as the walls. Photo by Marcus Hanschen.

LEFT: The privacy of the outdoor shower is enhanced with lattice walls and an adjacent bamboo tree. Photo by Marcus Hanschen.

POOL RETREAT IN THE MOUNTAINS
Design: Scott Lindenau, Studio B Architects
Photographs: Wayne Thom

Challenge: A protected outdoor space in a busy mixed-use resort neighborhood.
Result: A pool-focused courtyard that can't be seen from the street.

You don't have to live in an urban area to find yourself facing the challenge of how and where to create a private outdoor space. In this case, the building site in downtown Aspen, Colorado, was the primary hurdle. Located in a transitional mixed-use neighborhood of high-end homes, apartments, condominiums and even potential teardowns, the lot is bordered on three sides by streets and subject to the morning-to-night sounds of people and traffic. In many ways, it was the opposite of private. Architect Scott Lindenau's design for a courtyard with a pool at its center turned out to be the perfect solution.

The house is a series of low-profile volumes—a main house, guest house and garage—that together form a U-shape that defines a south-facing courtyard set off the street and practically invisible to passersby. With its expressive, sunny spaces and clear view of nearby Aspen Mountain, the courtyard is exactly what the owners wanted. They can host parties and enjoy the mountain setting without feeling as if they are in the middle of an active neighborhood—as indeed they are.

LEFT: Sail-like fabric canopies help shield the courtyard from intense summer sun without obstructing views of nearby Aspen Mountain. The canopies, which are supported by aluminum posts, can be easily removed and stored during the winter. Sections of light-colored gravel are inset with concrete paths that mark the transitions between indoors and out.

ABOVE: The main sections of the house embrace and define the courtyard. The building features a variety of materials, including cement board siding, zinc roofing, aluminum storefront windows, concrete and steel.

FACING: The focal point of the courtyard is a lap pool surrounded by a wood plinth adjacent to a slate firepit with built-in seating. The plinth is made from ipe, a weather-resistant Brazilian hardwood.

"The success of this project is that from the front of the house, you have no idea there's a courtyard unless you walk up and look in," Lindenau says. "The buildings buffer the courtyard against outside noise, and it does have the feel of a sanctuary."

The courtyard reveals a pared-down composition of wood, concrete and gravel, with a lap pool set into a plinth made from weather-resistant Brazilian ipe. The plinth rises out of the light-colored gravel, which is intersected at points by concrete paths that mark the transitions from indoors to outdoors.

A slate firepit with a built-in lounging bench provides a comfortable and warm place to relax, even during cooler days and nights. To shade the courtyard from the high-altitude sun, Lindenau attached steel trellises to the main house and stretched fabric canopies across the pool area. Held up by aluminum posts and easily removed for winter storage, the canopies effectively block sunlight without obstructing the views. The "native natural" landscape was designed in collaboration with Bluegreen Landscape Architects of Aspen.

ABOVE: The low-profile house blends into its diverse neighborhood, and the private areas of the property are contained within a courtyard at the back of the house, intentionally not visible from the street.

RIGHT: Tall windows on the house provide views down into the courtyard.

TRACT HOUSE POOL TRANSFORMATION
Design: Kraiger Thein and Roberto Concina
Photographs: Claudio Santini

Challenge: Revamp an out-of-date tract house pool and deck into a functional entertainment area that better relates to the rest of the property.

Result: A multifunctional pool-centered backyard with an easy connection to the main house.

Like many homes of its generation, this 1963 tract house in California's San Fernando Valley was in what architectural designer Kraiger Thein calls a "time warp. Although it was falling apart, it had been untouched. It felt like a museum piece."

The integrity of the original design motivated Thein and business partner Roberto Concina to embark on an extensive remodel to bring the house current without obliterating its history. Thein, who grew up in a similar house nearby, says he had a clear idea of how to update the home within minutes of walking through its front door. "Our goal was to work with the lines of the house, but it was immediately evident that we needed to do something about the lack of interaction between the indoors and outdoors," he says.

Although surrounded by an unappealing expanse of concrete and isolated from the house, the existing backyard pool became the driving force for the entire remodel. "It looked like someone had come along and just dropped

FACING ABOVE: The original form of the 1963 house is still intact but the exterior has been updated with matte Venetian plaster in a custom tomato-red color and clear anodized aluminum trim. The entire property is now enclosed with a cinder block wall clad in plaster the same color as the house.

FACING BELOW: Small round windows on the façade reinforce the circular theme of the home's updated elements. Trex planks at the front entry match the backyard pool deck.

ABOVE: The pool deck is now a retreat-like space conducive to social gatherings.

the pool into the backyard," Thein explains. "It had absolutely no relationship to the house."

The designers brought warmth and texture to the pool area by replacing the concrete with weather-resistant Trex decking in a shade of light grey brown. To visually break up the surface of the large deck, they installed a series of raised platforms: one has a gas firepit and plush pillow seating, another a

Jacuzzi, and yet another can be turned into a musical stage. Realizing they needed more room to do their work, they extended the deck farther out into the yard with a curved retaining wall that brings a feeling of enclosure to the space.

Then came the task of connecting the living room to the deck, accomplished by replacing the heavy sliding doors with automated glass panels that

fold open like an accordion at the touch of a button. Although more typically used in commercial buildings, the doors work beautifully in a residential setting.

With its gentle lines, creative arrangement of spaces and new textural materiality, the pool deck is now a desirable destination that, thanks to the mild southern California climate, can be used every month of the year.

ABOVE LEFT: Previously surrounded by an inhospitable expanse of concrete, the pool is now a more attractive place to gather. Trex boards cover the deck and platforms.

BOTTOM LEFT: A new cinder block retaining wall, installed to extend the deck farther out into the yard, complements the lines of the pool and is covered in the same plaster as the garden wall.

TOP: The sliding doors in the living room were replaced with electronic accordion glass doors that open at the touch of a button.

More typically used in commercial buildings, the doors work beautifully in a residential setting.

ABOVE: One of several gathering platforms on the deck, this one has a gas firepit, canvas pillows and sea grass cushions.

Spanish Colonial Ambience

Design: Erik Evens, KAA Design Group, and Frances E. Knight & Associates
Photographs: Brandie Handelmann

Challenge: A new house and landscape with an established appearance and a comprehensive but uncomplicated plan for a sloping, generously treed site.

Result: A house with a historic architectural reference and a terraced yard that incorporates water features both as focal points and transitions between spaces.

When people remark that this Los Angeles house looks as if it has been standing for decades, architect Erik Evens takes it as a compliment. Although constructed only several years ago, the Spanish Colonial–style dwelling is designed to look as if it has gracefully accommodated generations of occupants.

Evens, working closely with a team of colleagues at Los Angeles–based KAA Design Group, envisioned a house that was appropriate to its lush setting and would incorporate, rather than endanger, the numerous eucalyptus trees on the site. He even went so far as to configure the foundations for the eastern portion of the building so that they did not touch any root structures.

Having settled on a Spanish Colonial aesthetic that is historically appropriate to southern California, the clients requested an informal outdoor space with water features integral to the landscape. The nat-

ural slope of the yard readily accommodated terraces that progress down the length of the garden, passing through areas of differing function. The main upper terrace, adjacent to a loggia, is separated from a lower terrace by a fountain. From there, steps and paths move toward and along a simple rectangular pool, terminating at a pool house.

"The goal was a yard with easily defined layers," says Evens, who collaborated with landscape designer Frances Knight. "These layers create a sequential progression from the indoors to the outdoors, taking you from private interior spaces to more public outdoor spaces. The idea is that you meander out of the house and onto the main terrace, and then down the steps to the pool and pool house."

FACING ABOVE: A simple rectangular pool is the focal point of the terraced backyard. A smooth surface and a soft texture make sweetwater flagstone, locally quarried and used here on the pool deck, a good choice for areas where people go barefoot. The pool has a medium-dark plaster finish that in the sun emits a deep azure color.

FACING BELOW: Located at the far end of the yard and designed to differ from the main house both in style and materiality, the pool house resembles a rural building, with its low-profile façade of Santa Barbara sandstone rubble masonry and distressed Douglas fir trellis. The structure houses a full bath and shower, a changing room and a storage area.

LEFT: Clad in French limestone, a more formal counterpart to the sandstone used elsewhere on the property, the upper terrace is used for outdoor dining and entertaining and begins the progression down into the yard's lower spaces.

RIGHT: The layering of the garden, achieved with terraces and paths set into the lawn, is apparent from the upper terrace.

FACING LEFT: A wood-burning outdoor fireplace with a cast-stone surround and plaster hood occupies one end of the loggia. The loggia offers protection from wind and rain, making it usable year-round.

FACING RIGHT: A cascading fountain at the edge of the main terrace brings the soothing sound of water to the property. The fountain is Santa Barbara sandstone rubble masonry.

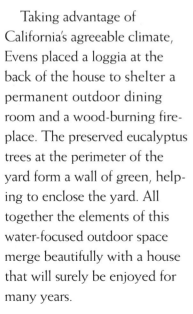

Taking advantage of California's agreeable climate, Evens placed a loggia at the back of the house to shelter a permanent outdoor dining room and a wood-burning fireplace. The preserved eucalyptus trees at the perimeter of the yard form a wall of green, helping to enclose the yard. All together the elements of this water-focused outdoor space merge beautifully with a house that will surely be enjoyed for many years.

SPACE FOR PLAY AND MEDITATION

Design: Douglas Teiger, Abramson Teiger Architects
Photographs: John Linden

Challenge: A backyard that would appeal to kids and also be a quiet, reflective space for adults.

Result: A streamlined pool deck clad in wood, and a backyard that reads like an extension of the house and is a reprieve from city life.

Before he undertook a remodel of his West Los Angeles backyard, architect Douglas Teiger thought carefully about what he wanted the new spaces to accomplish. At the top of his list was a more child-oriented play area for his three young boys. Also important was a quiet place to relax and meditate for himself and wife, Sabrina, who studies spiritual psychology.

The result is a pool/Jacuzzi and deck addition that connects architecturally to the house and has the feeling of an outdoor room. The garage, recently converted into a playroom, forms the main deck wood wall and supports a trellis that extends over the lounging platform. The materials were chosen for both warmth and durability: teak-stained redwood for the main wall, Douglas fir for the trellis and water-resistant Brazilian ipe for the deck and back wall. The pool and Jacuzzi are anchored at the far end by a neighboring

garage; the garage wall has been disguised with a row of trees and a low wall that can be used as a backrest.

Teiger was also concerned about safety and energy efficiency. To give his children a greater level of comfort when in the pool, he installed a bench eighteen inches below the surface that gives the kids something to hold on to when they are playing in the water. Solar panels on the playroom effectively heat the pool year-round; in fact, Teiger says he has never had to fire up the gas heating system.

"The goal was an outdoor room the children would enjoy and which would also evoke a strong sense of spirituality," Teiger says. "Now, the kids are in the pool every day, and Sabrina and I have a peaceful retreat just steps from the house."

LEFT: The original 1920s house has been transformed into a modern home. The redwood siding, which matches the wood used on parts of the pool deck, has been darkened with a teak stain.

ABOVE: The playroom, previously a garage, forms the main wall of the lounging platform and supports a trellis that extends over the deck and is tilted in reference to the lines of the house. Sliding glass doors at the family room and kitchen provide easy access to the new outdoor spaces, which are enjoyed as much by the owners' dog, Moca, as by the humans of the house.

FACING: Materials were chosen for their texture, color and water-resistance. The main wall is teak-stained redwood, the trellis is Douglas fir and the deck is teak-oiled ipe, a Brazilian hardwood. The low wall at the far end of the pool serves as a backrest and helps to visually break up the mass of the neighbor's garage, now camouflaged by a row of podocarpus trees.

ABOVE: The Jacuzzi is tucked into the far corner of the pool.

LEFT: A Buddha head floats above the low back wall, providing a focal point for meditating and relaxing, and clear glass tiles and plaster further establish the Zen mood of the pool. Here, the architect enjoys a quiet moment.

CONTEMPORARY POOL REMODEL

Design: Charles Bernstein, M. Charles Bernstein Architects
Photographs: Charles Bernstein

Challenge: Unite a home with its spacious but underutilized backyard, working around an existing pool.

Result: A reoriented pool that visually extends the house into the updated landscape, now arranged into well-defined outdoor living areas.

This Los Angeles–area property had plenty going for it: a desirable location, views of the Santa Monica Mountains and Pacific Ocean, and a pool. The problem was that the outdoor spaces didn't take full advantage of what the half-acre site had to offer.

The owners of the house hired architect Charles Bernstein to take the one-story tract house and its backyard from ho-hum to memorable. The first stage of the makeover involved an extensive remodel of the house itself. Bernstein designed a second-story addition, gave the façade a fresh look with modern materials and bold forms, and used large expanses of glass to connect the house to the yard and more precisely frame the views.

Once the house was completed, attention turned to reworking the backyard into a more functional and organized place to relax,

FACING: The remodeled house has a new second story and an updated exterior with metallic finishes and large windows. Now on axis with the addition, the pool extends from the house, giving the impression of a longer yard and drawing the eye toward the far end of the property.

LEFT: Square limestone pavers add a sense of order to the lawn and create a feeling of progression through the yard, which overlooks the Santa Monica Mountains and ocean beyond.

ABOVE: Simple but elegant landscaping elements were used to organize the newly configured backyard. Planters perched on limestone bases reflect the materiality of the patio and pavers.

gather and take in the scenery, with an emphasis on three main elements: pool, patio and lawn. The existing pool had been set at a ninety-degree angle to the house in a manner that interrupted the flow of the yard, making it feel smaller. Bernstein's solution was to move the pool, aligning it on axis with the addition. The pool's more straightforward placement fosters the illusion of a longer yard, one that embraces the views instead of turning away from them.

To give the owners a more direct indoor/outdoor experience, the architect suggested expanding the existing patio and adding a reflecting pond just off the master bedroom. The crowning touch is a canvas canopy at the far end of the pool that helps draw the eye from the house along the length of the yard. The canopy covers a sitting area that can be warmed by an adjacent firepit.

LEFT: A canvas canopy shelters a separate sitting area, and a freestanding concrete firepit provides warmth during cooler weather.

ABOVE: The patio features a reflecting pond inset with lime-stone stepping-stones.

RIGHT: French doors lead out onto the limestone patio, which has been expanded to increase the outdoor living space. Originally a tract-style house built in the 1970s, the remodeled home now interacts more directly with its setting.

WATER AT EVERY TURN

Design: John Cottle, CCY Architects
Photographs: Robert Millman
and John Cottle

Challenge: Intimately engage the house with its site by introducing water and enhancing the natural landscape.

Result: Man-made water features that flow through and around the home, and landscaped terraces and patios that connect indoor and outdoor spaces.

The owners of this mountain house near Vail, Colorado, wanted a contemporary home that would embrace the landscape, be filled with the sound of water and reflect the warmth and craftsmanship of traditional log architecture. Architect John Cottle met his clients' wishes with a series of nine simple cabin forms constructed with square-cut stacked Douglas fir timbers and stone and arranged in a gradual progression down the hillside. Most of the cabins have a sunny southern exposure—important for outdoor living at 8,500 feet. The cabins are connected with an African mahogany glass window-wall system that forms what Cottle describes as "connective tissue" that encourages the

occupants to view or step out into nature from every room.

"The transparency of the connective tissue makes the statement that, like great European hill towns, the magic is in between the cabins," he says. "Light plays between the cabins, and nature comes into and under and through the 'street.' It's a simple yet powerful idea."

The design brings water beneath, around and between the buildings. A heated indoor/outdoor lap pool can be used year-round, thanks to a glass transom that slides down like a garage door, bisecting the pool and closing it off for use during cold weather. Cottle and landscape architect Glenn Ellison collaborated on a

The property features a series of watercourses, outdoor terraces, gardens and a pool. Photo by Robert Millman.

landscaping concept that used large boulders to form ponds and waterfalls that, although manmade, look native to the terrain because of the care that went into placing them around the cabins. The boulders match the cabins' exterior stone, a visual effect that places the structures even more solidly into their environment and achieves the goal of seamless integration of land and architecture.

"When we design a house, we are careful to consider not just the site, but also how the senses are engaged," Cottle concludes. "With this house, you can hear water from almost every room, see the visual effect and movement of light bouncing off the water and into the house, and even detect the scent of water. No matter where you are in the house, you have a sensory connection to the outdoors."

Although man-made, the pond and stream appear native, thanks to the meticulous installation of boulders and plant material. The architect chose a spare, natural palette of reclaimed Douglas fir, African mahogany and Telluride Gold stone for the cabins. Photo by Robert Millman.

ABOVE: Located off the exercise room, the heated indoor/outdoor pool connects to an outdoor patio through sliding glass doors. The doors, in conjunction with a glass transom, make it possible to close off the pool during the winter.

The transom, framed in African mahogany to match the doors and windows, can be pulled down like a garage door. Photo by Robert Millman.

FACING LEFT: African mahogany window walls form "connective tissue" transitions between the cabins. Here, a man-made stream flows beneath a bridge. Photo by Robert Millman.

FACING ABOVE RIGHT: The living room projects out over a pond with Douglas fir support columns that engage with the water, literally placing the house into its landscape. Photo by John Cottle.

FACING BELOW RIGHT: Visible from the dining room, the waterfall is equipped with small lights that can be turned on at night for a dramatic dining experience. Photo by Robert Millman.

LUXURIOUS FLORIDA GETAWAY
Design: Koby Kirwin, SDG Landscape Architects
Photographs: Lori Hamilton

Challenge: Create private outdoor spaces between the main house and master suite, mitigate off-site noise, and block out a neighboring house.

Result: Divided exteriors and pool areas that form subtly linked zones, water features that buffer outside noise and a trellis/fountain wall system for privacy.

This lush property, located in a gated golf course community in Jupiter, Florida, is described by landscape architect Koby Kirwin as a residential resort, and his description is not an exaggeration. Designed for a couple whose travels in Asia fostered in them an appreciation for clean architectural lines and forms, this residence could easily pass for a high-end getaway for soothing frazzled nerves and calming the soul.

Kirwin, who with partner Tim Grey owns and operates SDG Landscape Architects, explains that his project came without budgetary constraints but did present key design parameters: an Asian-inspired aesthetic with a contemporary twist, low maintenance and a pared-down materiality. "The clients favored a clean-line approach to design, and they requested a limited variety of textures and materials, but ones that would be repeated around the entire house. We used a few different materials and then repeated them. The result is a peaceful, calming environment with a consistent theme."

This restraint in materials and textures resulted in a composition that flows easily from the main house to the exterior spaces. Dominating the site plan is a large pool divided into two sections: a master suite pool equipped with a spa and a main family pool. A gently arcing bridge visually separates the two in an arrangement of spaces that guarantees privacy in the master suite area and easy access to the main pool. The pools are also mechanically separate, allowing the master pool and spa to be heated for daily use while the main pool is heated only periodically.

Privacy in the master suite was important due to the presence of a neighboring house. A curving fountain wall and wood trellis gracefully block views into the spa from outside without compromising the integrity of the design or the views out to the golf course. "When you are in the master pool and spa, no one can see you. It's a very private setting," Kirwin notes. To mitigate noise from the golf course and a nearby road, Kirwin installed a water feature in the curving limestone fountain wall and placed a negative-edge fountain in the main pool. The sounds of falling and gushing water provide an effective buffer against off-site noise.

"This is an amphitheater-type space," Kirwin says. "It's very quiet and peaceful, very much like being at a resort."

FACING: A negative-edge fountain at the main pool serves dual purposes: it leads the eye from the end of the pool to a lake across from the house and helps block noise from the golf course.

ABOVE: The master suite pool and its peninsular spa are contained within a limestone-clad fountain wall topped with a curving wood trellis. The vine-covered trellis and fountain wall create a private setting without blocking natural light and closing off the space. Iridium glass mosaic tiles on the interior of the pool and the lower portion of the fountain walls shimmer in the sunlight.

LEFT: At night, the fountain wall seems to float above the water thanks to strategically placed lighting.

ABOVE LEFT: Custom-fabricated limestone scuppers on the fountain wall channel water to help buffer off-site noise, adding to the peacefulness of the space.

ABOVE RIGHT: Constructed of dead-fallen almendro, a rainforest wood, the trellis increases privacy and provides shade. Stained to match the home's casements and jambs, almendro was chosen for its ability to withstand the Florida climate and resist the fading effects of sunlight.

RIGHT: A cantilevered concrete bridge connects the master suite pool and spa to the main pool and decks. The bridge is softly arced and constructed without a handrail to complement the clean lines of the property. The black trim on the bridge is Mexican beach pebble and the stepping-stones are Mexican shellstone.

Creative Landscapes

INDIGENOUS VERMONT LODGE

Design: David Sellers,
Sellers and Company
Photographs: Carolyn Bates

Challenge: A complicated site and the wish for a house that highlights the beauty of natural materials and has a clear relationship to the setting.

Result: A modern-day wood and stone lodge that connects to the land with flexible, year-round outdoor living spaces.

Located on what architect David Sellers describes as "an amazingly difficult site" in rural Vermont, this contemporary interpretation of a historical lodge takes its cues straight from the environment.

After studying the steeply sloping site, Sellers presented his clients with a plan that would follow the contours of the land rather than reshape them to fit the house. The result is a building and accompanying outdoor spaces that appear as if the land has risen around them.

The sheltered front of the house digs into the hillside and increases in height as the treed slope falls away toward the sunnier southwest exposure at the back, creating the visual effect of a building emerging from the ground. In fact, in some places the roofline is so near to the ground that in the winter, snow accumulates around the roof edges, practically engulfing the structure. Out of respect for the wildness of the setting, Sellers preserved as many trees as possible. The trees that did have to

FACING: The home's undulating slate roof hugs the ground at the front elevation and in some places is only one or two feet high, which in the winter allows snow on the ground to join with snow on the roof, further camouflaging the structure.

ABOVE: The back of the house rises up to greet the forested setting, which has been organized with terraces made from stone collected during excavation. The siding is oiled cedar.

be moved during construction were stored and later relocated.

The owners wanted outdoor spaces that could be used year-round. Taking into account the length of the Vermont winters, Sellers responded with a design that accommodates all seasons: an outdoor fireplace, a hot tub built into the rocks below a porch, a separate sauna accessed by a narrow walkway set into the trees, and decks that meet up with the forest.

To further emphasize the indigenous qualities of the house, Sellers incorporated materials found on the site into the architecture. For example, the fireplace and porch feature stone unearthed during excavation, the walkway to the sauna has a curved railing made from the branches of local trees and the decks are supported by thick maple tree trunks left in their natural state. "We set aside an inventory of interesting trunks and branches to use both indoors and outdoors," he says. "This gave us a zero-cost supply of materials and a variety of curvilinear possibilities that enhanced the organic feel of the house."

ABOVE: A walkway connects the outdoor fireplace and porch to the sauna. The curved rail is made from the branches of maple trees found on the site.

LEFT: The sauna bench was crafted from a maple log cut from the site.

ABOVE LEFT: The steep slope provided the opportunity to extend the house right into the forest. The upper and lower decks are supported by maple tree trunks taken from the site and left in their natural state, and ample overhangs help protect the outdoor spaces during inclement weather.

ABOVE RIGHT: An outdoor fireplace heats the patio during the winter. The fireplace and patio stone were taken from the site during construction.

BELOW RIGHT: The steepness of the slope precluded a foundation for the sauna, constructed of recycled blackboard slate and tucked into the trees. In place of a foundation, the architect set the building on stainless steel legs fixed into holes drilled into the natural stone ledge.

COLORFUL CALIFORNIA EICHLER

Design: Michelle Van de Voorde, Elemental Design

Photographs: Gregory Case

Challenge: Update the worn-out exteriors without sacrificing space and turn the yard into a series of zones that reference the interiors.

Result: A playful outdoor space that features the colors and patterns found inside the home, as well as separate areas for dining, relaxing and recreation.

Like many others of its kind, this California Eichler had been lovingly remodeled inside, but its outdoor spaces suffered from dilapidated fencing, rotted decking and tired concrete. When the owners, two software engineers with a penchant for the whimsical and an appreciation for cutting-edge design, hired landscape architect Michelle Van de Voorde, the discussion turned to ways to relate the exterior spaces to the patterns and colors found indoors. "We wanted to tie the outdoors to the indoors," Van de Voorde explains. "In this case, it made sense to play with the colors, patterns and textures inside the house and bring them outside as a complement to the interiors."

The highlights of the new outdoor space are two curving concrete privacy walls, one cobalt blue, the other a terra-cotta red, and a seafoam green concrete path that meanders through the property, linking the various elements. A patio outside the master bedroom features a grid pattern that mimics the colors and pattern of an inside wall; similarly, the blue privacy wall continues the blue of an interior wall. This pronounced indoor/outdoor connection makes the exteriors feel like true extensions of the interiors, and the update as a whole took the three-sided yard from boring to dynamic.

The owners also requested a special play area for their young daughter, and Van de Voorde responded with a prefab playhouse tucked into a corner of the yard. The green path passes by the playhouse and, to the child, is reminiscent of the famous Yellow Brick Road. "We wanted to make the yard fun for the little girl, and she loves this path," the architect says. Materials were limited to concrete and Trex decking, giving the outdoor spaces a consistent and streamlined appearance. Thoughtfully restored, this Eichler gem is now beautiful inside and out.

FACING: The privacy walls
are made from concrete
block covered in stucco and
then painted. The walls
replaced the old fencing.

ABOVE: The outdoor dining
patio features a curving concrete privacy wall painted the
same blue as an interior wall,
visible through the far window.
The patio is stamped concrete.

LEFT: A shoji screen creates a niche for a future hot tub, and the yellow and terra-cotta-colored grid on the master bedroom patio corresponds to a similar pattern on an interior wall. The patio is concrete with a colored hardener.

ABOVE: The front entrance is separated from the outdoor dining patio by the terra-cotta-colored privacy wall.

ALL PHOTOS: A seafoam green concrete path meanders through the property, at one point even bisecting a Trex deck located in a back section of the yard (the architect poured the path first and then built the deck up around it).

INNOVATIVE AND ECONOMICAL ROOFTOP ROOM

Design: Stephen Dynia, Stephen Dynia Architects
Photographs: Cameron Neilson

Challenge: Work around the confines of a budget, a tight neighborhood and a restricted building envelope to create a stylish and private outdoor space.

Result: A rooftop living room filled with economical materials used in out-of-the-ordinary ways.

Although it has enviable views of a nearby ski hill, this site in downtown Jackson, Wyoming, was restricted by a small building envelope and square footage limitations. Architect Stephen Dynia, who purchased the property for himself, devised a perfect solution: a pair of loft-like "cube" apartments with compact 750-square-foot floor plans.

Dynia, who lives in one of the apartments and rents out the other, wasn't content to stop at the buildings; he also wanted an outdoor space that would look and feel like an extension of the interior. Here again he encountered an obstacle: there were few opportunities for a ground-level yard. This time he applied his creativity vertically, turning the roof into an outdoor room.

Situated at a relatively moderate elevation of 6,200 feet, Jackson is not as high as some mountain towns but its long winters can make outdoor living a daunting proposition. "No one else had done this up here," Dynia acknowledges. "The concept of an outdoor room on a rooftop presented a lot of unknowns. I had to take into consideration how much of the year I would be able to use the space and how the wind, sun and snow would affect it."

Dynia's revamped roof reveals his flair for dreaming up unusual ways to use materials. Accessed by a fire escape–like stair on the side of the building, the room is sheltered on three sides with a willow stick privacy fence. A rustic counterpart to the modern apartment, the height of the fence "makes you feel like the ski hill is coming right down into the garden," Dynia explains. He used rubber flooring tiles in lieu of a wood deck for a number of reasons: they are economical, easy to install, won't wear on the roof's rubber membrane as a wood deck might do and form a protective surface.

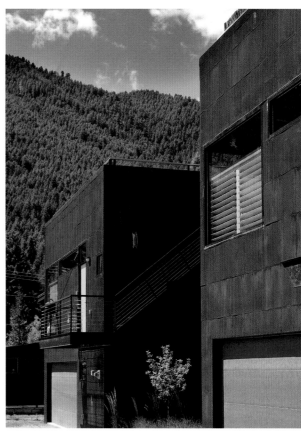

ABOVE: The "cubes" are clad in rusted sheet metal that, from a distance, resembles wood but requires no maintenance. The garage and entry doors are painted in vibrant colors to contrast with the metal. A fire escape–style steel stair provides easy access to the roof.

RIGHT: A willow stick privacy fence on three sides of the roof effectively blocks out neighboring houses without impeding views to the ski hill. Long-lasting rubber floor tiles were chosen for their affordability and because they will not wear on the roof's rubber membrane as a wood structure might. The large elliptical planters are made from zinc and filled with ponytail grass.

ABOVE: The room reveals the versatility of natural and man-made materials—all of them budget-conscious. The architect built a simple seating bench with redwood planks placed on stacks of extra rubber floor tiles. The coffee table reveals what can be accomplished with a little research and a lot of ingenuity. The architect found a tempered glass shower stall that had been sized incorrectly, bought it for just $50, and turned it into a table top supported by automotive jack stands.

FACING ABOVE: A store-bought metal planter filled with water serves as a low-cost design element. Ornamental grasses bring soft color to the space and help define the zones of the room.

FACING BELOW: A side bench/plant shelf was crafted from a piece of galvanized sheet metal left over after construction. The slatted fence allows for easy snow removal and is inset with vertical extensions that in the future will support a fabric shade canopy. The slats are pine and the top edge of the fence is redwood.

FACING RIGHT: Dynia can create instant ambience by placing floating oil lamps into one of the water-filled planters.

Keeping his budget in mind, Dynia searched for ways to give old materials new life. He found a tempered glass shower stall that had been sized incorrectly, bought it for just $50, and turned it into a coffee table. Automotive jack stands became the coffee table legs, and the benches are supported by stacks of extra rubber tiles.

Although Dynia enjoys his rooftop room primarily during the summer and early fall, on a sunny winter day, when the wind is calm and the sky is as blue as it gets, he would agree there's no better place to be.

UP IN THE TREES
Design: John Cottle, CCY Architects
Photographs: John Cottle

Challenge: Maximize the views and sun exposure on a shaded north-facing site without negatively affecting the land.

Result: A low-impact tree-level platform deck that provides a dramatic link to the natural environment.

Not all landscapes present straightforward opportunities for usable exterior spaces. Architect John Cottle worked with his clients to find a solution for this steep and thickly wooded north-facing site near Telluride, Colorado, that offers a unique—and perhaps unusual—way to experience the mountain setting. They just happen to be thirty-five feet off the ground when they do so.

Before designing this platform in the sky, Cottle wrestled with the challenges of the slope and how to create an intimate connection between the house and the outdoors. "This site presented so few traditional ways to connect with nature," he explains. "So we had to come up with an unusual way to make it work."

Using the slope and dense forest to his advantage, Cottle designed a square platform that terminates at the end of a slender forty-five-foot-long walkway accessed off the living room. Aptly named the "Bird's Nest," the structure, which is thirty-five feet off the ground at its highest point, juts straight out into the upper reaches of

the trees and, though perhaps not for the faint of heart, offers a powerful treetop encounter. The structure even sways when the wind blows in a fine-tuned mimicry of the movement of the aspens and evergreens, and the bridge deflects slightly with each step to further enhance that movement. The platform also catches the sun exposure that wouldn't reach a deck located adjacent to the house.

To minimize the impact of construction and save trees, the main steel support column and deck platform were flown in by helicopter and then attached. Used for small gatherings and as a tranquil place to sit and take in the mountain scenery, the platform is equipped with a small gas firepit and stainless steel benches that can be flipped down for seating or flipped up to make more room for standing.

Says Cottle, "When you see the structure from inside the house, it encourages you to psychologically inhabit the forest more deeply than you normally would. And of course when you're out there it's magical."

FACING: The main components of the Bird's Nest were flown in by helicopter and assembled on-site, which allowed for precise placement in the trees. At its high-est point, the structure is thirty-five feet off the ground.

ABOVE: A gas firepit set into a concrete tub accented with black lava rock warms the platform during cooler weather. Stainless steel benches at the perimeter of the platform can be lowered for seating or flipped up to make more room for standing.

ABOVE: Visible from the master bathroom, the Bird's Nest stretches deep into the aspen and evergreen forest.

FACING: The forty-five-foot-long walkway extends from the main living space to an eleven-square-foot platform deck. The open railing is a combination of traditional carbon and stainless steel, and the walkway and deck platform are open steel grating.

COLLECTION OF CULTIVATED SPACES
Design: Stephen Dynia, Stephen Dynia Architects
Photographs: Ron Johnson, Paul Warchol and Stephen Dynia

Challenge: Preserve the beauty of a rural setting while creating outdoor spaces that correspond to the architecture of the buildings.

Result: Organized, self-contained courtyard gardens and lawns that encourage an intimate interaction with the outdoors without overpowering the native landscape.

The owners of this forty-eight-acre property near Jackson, Wyoming, were drawn to its pastoral beauty and wanted a house with outdoor spaces that would both enhance and preserve the meadows and woodlands.

The couple hired architect Stephen Dynia, who conceived of a compound-like arrangement of buildings that includes a main house, guest house and horse barn. Each structure pays homage to the region's agricultural vernacular and engages with the site through a series of cultivated outdoor spaces. These spaces are self-contained within the native landscape with boundaries that mark where cultivation ends and the undeveloped meadow resumes. For example, manicured lawns are bordered by a sharp

line of concrete that separates them from the wild grasses beyond, and a stone wall partially encloses a southeast-facing courtyard garden, setting it apart from the entry drive.

The buildings are a contemporary interpretation of the ranch structures common to the area, Dynia says. The Z-shaped main house appears to settle into the site, and its rising and falling roof forms are reminiscent of old farmhouses that "sag" to the ground as they age, he points out. A two-tiered viewing platform anchors one side of the main house and features a spiral stair that leads to the top platform, which overlooks stands of cottonwood trees and opens up views of the Grand Tetons. Desiring water on the property, the owners diverted

LEFT: The west elevation of the main house features sloping roof forms reminiscent of the region's old ranch buildings. The roof is rusted Corten steel and the siding is mahogany. Photo by Paul Warchol.

ABOVE: Manicured lawns visually extend the interiors into the setting and are bordered with strips of concrete to separate them from the adjacent native landscape. Photo by Stephen Dynia.

existing agricultural canals to form three ponds that attract a variety of wildlife.

The home, with its combination of manicured outdoor sanctuaries and untamed stretches of land, reflects Dynia's passion for architecture that honors the natural environment and takes as its cues historical references provided by early buildings. "I always try to find ways to design houses that are contextual," he says. "The context drives everything—in this case, how the house relates to its setting, and how the outdoor spaces work to extend the house into nature."

FAR LEFT: The house wraps around a southeast-facing courtyard filled with grasses and separated from the entry drive by a stone wall. Photo by Ron Johnson.

ABOVE: Existing agricultural canals were diverted to create three ponds on the site. The ponds attract a variety of wildlife, including trumpeter swans. A concrete border marks where the cultivated lawn ends and the meadow resumes. Photo by Stephen Dynia.

LEFT: The courtyard garden is bordered by a wall made of Montana moss rock. Photo by Ron Johnson.

LEFT: One side of the main house is anchored by a two-tiered viewing tower, constructed with a painted steel frame attached to a support wall clad in copper shingles. A spiral staircase leads to the top platform, which overlooks a pond and has views of the Teton mountain range. An outdoor fireplace at the base of the tower makes the patio an inviting place to gather. Photo by Paul Warchol.

ABOVE: The Z-shaped floor plan of the main house forms sunny, intimate courtyards filled with orderly plantings of grasses and perennials divided by sandstone gravel paths. Photo by Ron Johnson.

MAGICAL GARDEN ON A BUDGET
Design: Matt Charlot
Photographs: Marcus Hanschen

Challenge: A tight budget, a "crooked" uphill site and the desire for privacy in an urban neighborhood.

Result: An affordable terraced yard that accommodates the difficult site, showcases the beauty of salvaged redwood and shields the house from the neighbors.

Before it was transformed into what landscape designer Matt Charlot describes as a magical garden, the backyard of this Oakland, California, house was a tangle of blackberry bushes that threatened to consume the unwieldy uphill site. For this project, his own house, Charlot applied the same principles he employs in his practice: use salvaged materials as much as possible and build the design into the terrain, working with it rather than against it.

Charlot had a tight budget and knew that removing old materials from the yard would cost money, so he reused them whenever possible; for example, he recycled the existing stone and concrete retaining walls instead of hauling them away in favor of new materials. He searched the Web for construction materials, hitting the jackpot on Craigslist with a listing for free redwood fencing salvaged from an old naval base. The tossed-aside fencing found new life in a perimeter trellis system that helps shade the yard and shields it from adjacent

structures, one of which is a three-story apartment building.

The yard rises steeply from the house with an eighteen-foot gain in elevation from bottom to top. And it was oddly angled, giving the impression, Charlot says, "that you would fall into a corner of the yard from the top. It just felt askew." He solved this problem by straightening the planes of the site, cutting and filling them in and essentially redistributing the earth to give the yard a more uniform appearance. To create well-defined zones, he contained the terraces with retaining walls fronted with pieces of redwood left over from other jobs. He experimented with the redwood, seeing how far he could bend it into the curves that now give the yard its organic character.

"Before the remodel, the yard was uninteresting and unreachable in many spots," Charlot says. "The design is meant to envelop you and funnel you up into the yard. There is now a sense of wanting to travel through the space."

ABOVE: The yard is now a private haven within an urban setting.

FACING: Located in the uppermost section of the yard, a curtained pergola draws the eye up through the space and serves as a separate outdoor room. The fence was made from salvaged redwood panels.

ABOVE: The perimeter trellis system was constructed with redwood fencing salvaged from an old naval base. In time, the trellises will be covered in trailing plants, further enclosing the space.

ABOVE RIGHT: The designer organized the previously untamed yard into well-defined terraces.

BELOW RIGHT: The recirculating fountain is the visual starting point for the progression up the hill. The top and bottom curving pieces are redwood to match the retaining walls, and the dark portion is black river rock. A small flame comes out of the center disk.

FACING: The designer experimented with bending pieces of redwood, pushing the material to its limit. Redwood is flexible enough to withstand such treatment, and the results are organic in appearance and less formal than square retaining walls.

NEW YORK CITY HIDEAWAYS
Design: Kate Ewald, Blue Angel Garden Design
Photographs: Kate Ewald

Challenge: Comfortable, inviting out-door spaces and gardens in the middle of New York City.

Result: Rooftop and terrace gardens designed for privacy and retreat.

If New York City doesn't bring to mind images of peacefulness and serenity, think again. The urban gardens and outdoor rooms designed by Kate Ewald of Blue Angel Garden Design truly are spaces for retreat and relaxation—not an easy task in a city of millions.

Ewald, herself a native New Yorker, takes what she describes as "blank" spaces—unused rooftops, empty terraces, forgotten patios—and turns them into getaways for clients who want to take the edge off city living. "Many of my clients like to spend time outdoors but don't have country homes," Ewald says. "I suggest an outdoor room with lots of plants—a rooftop terrace can become a person's 'Hamptons' with the right plants and features. My clients also understand that investing in outdoor spaces is a financially savvy move."

It could be said that Ewald specializes in illusions—gardens that seem bigger than they are, or feel like they are somewhere other than in the middle of a city. "When someone tells me he has a 400-square-foot living room

and a 400-square-foot patio, I point out that connecting the living room and patio would translate into an 800-square-foot living space."

Ewald's main goal is comfort, with an emphasis on basic materials such as stone and wood. "In a city, it's important that you feel as comfortable outside as you would inside," she explains. To achieve this, she designs gardens appointed with long-lasting furniture and filled with lush plants to bring privacy and the sought-after

ABOVE: This bedroom patio was turned into an inviting outdoor space with the simple addition of plants and a chaise lounge. Vines and trailing roses help disguise the open railing, making the patio feel more secure.

FACING: Planter boxes of various heights have been stacked in tiers to form a wall of greenery on this spacious rooftop terrace. A cedar pergola shelters an outdoor dining table and chairs.

ABOVE: Lush ornamental grasses flourish in their rooftop home and a latticed cedar pergola permits sunlight to fall onto the patio.

ABOVE FACING: Stacked planters give the space the feel of a country garden and a cedar fence ensures privacy.

BELOW FACING: The designer retained the openness of this Greenwich Village terrace but added interest and color with a cedar lattice-trellis structure inset with mirrors to foster the illusion of an expanded space. Bluestone-clad planters can double as seating, and the patio pavers are bluestone set in sand and edged with river stone.

"country" ambience. For one rooftop garden, she stacked planter boxes of different heights to create a wall of plants, then installed a cedar pergola to shade and enclose an outdoor dining room. For an apartment with a northeast-facing bedroom patio, she used vines to camouflage the open railing and placed a wood chaise lounge amid containers of ornamental grasses; the patio is now the perfect place to greet the day. For a terrace off the back of a Greenwich Village brownstone, she built a cedar trellis structure inset with mirrors to give the impression that the space continues beyond the yard.

In spreading the word about the untapped potential of urban spaces, Ewald is bringing her message of green to the denizens of this East Coast concrete jungle.

RESOURCES

ARCHITECTS AND DESIGNERS

TREVOR ABRAMSON
Abramson Teiger Architects
8924 Lindblade Street
Culver City, CA 90232
(310) 838-8998
www.abramsonteiger.com

ALDO ANDREOLI
Sanba International
2675 West Highway 89A, Suite 449
Sedona, AZ 86336
(928) 282-3755
www.sanba.com

MARIA BARMINA
Mark English Architects
250 Columbus Avenue, Suite 200
San Francisco, CA 94133
(415) 391-0186
www.markenglisharchitects.com

CHARLES BERNSTEIN
M. Charles Bernstein Architects
904 Pacific Avenue
Venice, CA 90291
(310) 452-1560
www.mcharlesbernstein.com

BLUEGREEN LANDSCAPE ARCHITECTS
300 South Spring Street, Suite 202
Aspen, CO 81611
(970) 429-7499
www.bluegreenaspen.com

MICHAEL CHACON
MAC Architecture/Construction
251 Whitclem Court
Palo Alto, CA 94306
(650) 796-8895
www.mac-archcon.com

ROSS CHAPIN
Ross Chapin Architects
P.O. Box 230
Langley, WA 98260
(360) 221-2373
www.rosschapin.com

MATT CHARLOT
1522 Holman
Oakland, CA 94610
(510) 919-5354
www.mattcharlot.com

JOSHUA COGGESHALL
Cog Work Shop
6000 Monte Vista Street
Highland Park, CA 90042
(323) 719-2265
www.cogworkshop.com

JOHN COTTLE
CCY Architects
P.O. Box 529
Basalt, CO 81621
(970) 927-4925
www.ccyarchitects.com

STEPHEN DYNIA
Stephen Dynia Architects
P.O. Box 4356
1135 Maple Way
Jackson, WY 83001
(307) 733-3766
www.dynia.com

GLENN ELLISON
Land Designs By Ellison
P.O. Box 1259
Avon, CO 81620
(970) 949-1700
www.landdesignsbyellison.com

MARK ENGLISH
Mark English Architects
250 Columbus Avenue, Suite 200
San Francisco, CA 94133
(415) 391-0186
www.markenglisharchitects.com

ERIK EVENS
KAA Design Group, Inc.
4201 Redwood Avenue
Los Angeles, CA 90066
(310) 821-1400
www.kaadesigngroup.com

KATE EWALD
Blue Angel Garden Design
41 West 16th Street, #5A
New York, NY 10011
(212) 727-3725
www.blueangeldesign.com

MICHAEL FOLONIS
Michael W. Folonis and Associates
1731 Ocean Park Boulevard
Santa Monica, CA 90405
(310) 450-4011
www.folonisarchitect.com

JOSÉ FONTIVEROS
MARIANA BOCTOR
Sintesi Design
1119 Colorado Avenue, #2
Santa Monica, CA 90401
(310) 394-9496
www.sintesidesign.com

FRANCES E. KNIGHT & ASSOCIATES
1386 Monument Street
Pacific Palisades, CA 90272
(310) 454-6746

RON GODFREDSEN
DANNA SIGAL
Godfredsen Sigal Architects
1501 Main Street, #203
Venice, CA 90291
(310) 664-0302
www.gsa.archinoid.net

TIM GORDON
BOORA Architects, Inc.
720 SW Washington Street, Suite 800
Portland, OR 97205
(503) 226-1575
www.boora.com

DANIEL JOHNSON
Design-Build-Studio Architecture
1280 Turnpike Road
Norwich, VT 05055
(802) 649-5533

KOBY KIRWIN AND TIM GREY
SDG Landscape Architects, Inc.
1865 Veterans Park Drive, #204
Naples, FL 34110
(239) 598-4707
www.sdgla.com

TONI LEWIS
MARC SCHOEPLEIN
Lewis Schoeplein Architects
10590 ½ West Pico Boulevard
Los Angeles, CA 90064
(310) 842-8620
www.lewisschoeplein.com

SCOTT LINDENAU
Studio B Architects
555 North Mill Street
Aspen, CO 81611
(970) 920-9428
www.studiobarchitects.net

BILL NICHOLAS
Nicholas Budd Dutton Architects
7958 West 3rd Street
Los Angeles, CA 90048
(323) 653-0226
www.nbdarchitects.com

RICK HARLAN SCHNEIDER
PETROS ZOUZOULAS
Inscape Studio
1215 Connecticut Avenue NW, Third Floor
Washington, DC 20036
(202) 416-0333
www.inscapestudio.com

DAVID SELLERS
Sellers and Company
P.O. Box 288
Warren, VT 05674
(802) 496-2787
www.sellersandcompany.com

JOHN SOFIO
Built, Inc.
7257 Beverly Boulevard
Los Angeles, CA 90036
(323) 857-0409
www.builtinc.com

DOUGLAS TEIGER
Abramson Teiger Architects
8924 Lindblade Street
Culver City, CA 90232
(310) 838-8998
www.abramsonteiger.com

KRAIGER THEIN
ROBERTO CONCINA
Thein-Concina Architectural Design
   and Development
350 North Spaulding Avenue, #3
Los Angeles, CA 90036
(323) 937-2424

MICHELLE VAN DE VOORDE
Elemental Design
1200 Blue Ridge Drive
Boulder Creek, CA 95006
(831) 338-1709
www.elementaldesign.com

PHOTOGRAPHERS

DAVID ADAMSON
HARRIET ROBINSON
Lone Pine Pictures
6944 Langdon Avenue
Van Nuys, CA 91406
(818) 785-9313
www.lonepinepictures.com

BERNARD ANDRÉ
2 Medway Road
Woodside, CA 94062
(650) 851-4630
www.bernardandre.com

CAROLYN BATES
20 Caroline Street
Burlington, VT 05401
(802) 862-5386
www.carolynbates.com

DEBORAH BIRD
(323) 493-8963

BLACKY'S STUDIO
blacky@blackystudio.de

GREGORY CASE
415-112 North Mary Avenue, #358
Sunnyvale, CA 94086
(408) 248-9721
www.gregorycase.com

STEPHANIE GROSS
795 Falling Rock Drive
Amherst, VA 24521
(434) 962-2019
stephanie@ntelos.net

LORI HAMILTON
3541 Quails Walk
Bonita Springs, FL 34134
(239) 595-5717

BRANDIE HANDELMANN
KAA Design Group, Inc.
4201 Redwood Avenue
Los Angeles, CA 90066
(310) 821-1400
www.kaadesigngroup.com

MARCUS HANSCHEN
25 Twain Avenue
Berkeley, CA 94708
(415) 595-8676
www.marcushanschen.com

STAR JENNINGS
921 East 49½ Street
Austin, TX 78751
(512) 963-9666

RON JOHNSON
Ron Johnson Photography
3301 Osceola Street
Denver, CO 80212
(303) 458-0288

JOHN LINDEN
John Edward Linden Architectural
  Photographer
4207 Michelangelo Avenue
Woodland Hills, CA 91364
(818) 888-8544
www.johnlindenphotographs.com

ROBERT MILLMAN
P.O. Box 3566
Aspen, CO 81612
(970) 948-8423
www.robertmillman.com

CAMERON R. NEILSON
P.O. Box 8485
Jackson, WY 83002
(307) 734-9775
www.theseenphoto.com

MICHAEL O'CALLAHAN
Michael O'Callahan Photography
80 The Alameda
San Anselmo, CA 94960
(415) 552-3686

DAN REDMOND
Redmond Architectural Photography
861 North Jefferson Street
Arlington, VA 22205
(703) 812-9565
www.danredmond.com

MARCO RICCA
(212) 529-2220
marcoricca@mac.com
www.homepage.mac.com/marcoricca/portfolio

CLAUDIO SANTINI
12915 Greene Avenue
Los Angeles, CA 90066
(310) 578-7919
www.claudiosantini.com

SALLY SCHOOLMASTER
7111 NE Morris Street
Portland, OR 97213
(503) 288-1458

WAYNE THOM
2458 Robert Road
Rowland Heights, CA 91748
(909) 595-6671
www.waynethom.com

PAUL WARCHOL
Paul Warchol Photography, Inc.
224 Centre Street, 5th Floor
New York, NY 10013
(212) 431-3461
www.warcholphotography.com